NEVER LET ANYONE DRAW THE BLINDS

The autobiography

of

Lottie Martin

1899–1920

edited by Julie O'Neill

Published by Paula Hill 1985
Reprinted 1985
Second edition 1989
Reprinted 1996

ISBN 0 9510405 1 0

Copies available from:

Ms P A Pardoe
1 The Square
Bramcote Lane
Wollaton
Nottingham
NG8 2AJ

Printed in England by:–
Technical Print Services Ltd,
Brentcliffe Ave, Carlton Road,
Nottingham NG3 7AG.

CONTENTS

ILLUSTRATIONS

ACKNOWLEDGEMENTS

We would like to thank many people for their help and support in preparing this book for publication. The Nottinghamshire County Council Leisure Services Department for their support, in particular the staff of the Local Studies library at Angel Row, Nottingham for their help and for giving permission to reproduce photographs 4,8,10,11,12,14,15,16,17; Dr Steven Wallwork for reading the draft and sharing with us his knowledge of Beeston places and people; Chris Richards for designing the cover and the staff of Technical Print Services Limited for their advice and patience.

We would also like to thank the following for giving permission to reproduce photographs:

Beeston and District Local History Society- 2,3,5,7,20
Brewhouse Yard Museum, Nottingham - 13
Imperial War Museum, London - 19
Alan Oxley, Author of *Barton* - 9
People's Palace (Glasgow Museums) - 18

Last, but not least, we remain grateful to the following who provided sponsorship for the first edition:

J Barlow and Co. (Nottingham) Ltd
Bass Worthington
Bell Fruit Manufacturing Company Ltd
The Boots Company PLC
Broxtowe Borough Council
Plessey
Supreme Rubber Stamp Company

Paula Hill
Julie O' Neill

INTRODUCTION

Lottie Martin was born on Good Friday 1899 in Beeston, Nottinghamshire, the daughter of a foundry worker – the fifth child in a family of seven. She grew up and lived in and around Beeston for the rest of her life.

In one sense Lottie was a very ordinary person who lived a very ordinary life. Nothing special happened to her that did not happen to many others of her time. At the same time she was also a very extraordinary person in that she recognised the value of her own experiences to her own family and took the trouble to write them down, and to do it very well.

I first read Lottie's autobiography when it was loaned to the Centre for Local History at the University of Nottingham by her grand-daughter and I was immediately impressed by the power of her writing and her ability to evoke the spirit of an era. In her story, sometimes amusing, sometimes moving, Lottie takes us through her experiences of the events and atmosphere of the first twenty years of the twentieth century. Best of all she takes us on this journey not with the wisdom of hindsight but with the eyes and preoccupations of the child and young woman that she was at the time.

Lottie headed her writings "For my children", never intending them for publication, but hers is a story which must have been shared by many others of her generation and deserves to be shared with the generations of her children and grandchildren.

The title is my choice because in a very moving episode she exhorts us "Never let anyone draw the blinds when I am gone" and it occurred to me that, in leaving her written experiences, she has herself ensured that the blinds were left open on her life for us all to share. I hope, therefore, that in reading this book and seeing how interesting an ordinary life can seem generations later, others will be encouraged to set down their own experiences and leave the blinds open on their lives too.

Julie O'Neill

"There was Sarah Ann seated with Tom and Liz at her side smiling like little angels and I, a little to the side, with a sad and sulky face."

Chapter 1 MY CHILDHOOD 1899 – 1909

I was born at 8 Greyhound Yard, High Road, Beeston on March 31st 1899. Good Friday fell on this particular day and as a child I heard many people say that she will see sorrow, born on this saddest of days in the year. For myself I never look on this day in the calendar as being more sorrowful than any other for was there not the wonderful day of resurrection to follow? This to my mind outweighed the day of suffering and grief.

My most vivid early memory was the coronation of Edward the Seventh and the celebrations of victory of our troops in South Africa over the Boers – reasons enough for the whole nation to rejoice which it did on 3rd July 1902. I shall never forget that glorious day. Discarded were the khaki uniforms which had been worn for the first time by troops in action: once again the men marched through the streets in the splendour of their red jackets. Drays were used as platforms to present different tableaux, banners of the various lodges and clubs, every school child over the age of three and under thirteen carried a union jack, quite a few adults were dressed as nurses and 'Lord Roberts' was there on a white horse. How everyone cheered as he went by, but the replica of Kruger was met with boos and cat calls as he was led to his doom; the people burned him that evening along with the roasting of the ox. The day was something to be remembered.

I was not allowed to walk the whole route but I remember plainly my mother lifting me on to one of the passing horse-drawn drays which were carrying other small children so I finished the walk along with the other children. We were given tea in Nether Street Schools and on leaving every child was presented with a mug inscribed with the lettering and picture of a soldier and a sailor with the words 'Peace' 'Celebration' 'South African War 1899 – 1902'. I thought the soldiers, two of them who stood one each side of the iron gates, were the biggest men I had ever seen, probably because they were wearing bearskins on their heads and this would make them look considerably taller than they actually were. I presume they must have been Guards and their glorious resplendant uniform was a sight any child would remember. Another thing imprinted on my mind was the sight of my young brother then eight months old. We had left him in the care of a little old lady by the name of Fox who we always called Tilly and she had regaled his very young appetite with blackcurrant jam. His face was covered with this sticky, coloured substance, but on our return he was quickly wiped clean and put to my mother's breast for in those days no mother would degrade herself by putting her child on the bottle. Besides, did not cow's milk cost money (about three half pence a pint) and this expenditure was to be avoided at all costs. Often the poor mother would suffer for many of them fed their children until they were two or even three years old.

There were many cases of ricketts in children and children died too. Our family had its share of death and illness. My mother and father had married in 1886 and the following year Thomas was born. I understand that he was fair-haired and blue-eyed like my father but he only lived until he was three years old dying through the effects of measles which took a great toll of life in those days. My mother made a great trouble of this. For years she treasured his little vest and shoes and even when I was a small child I remember the memoriam picture and the pathetic verse which hung in a frame on the wall of the room in which we lived. My eldest sister Sarah Ann was born in 1890 and two years later Emily, then in 1895 another girl, Lily who was so named because of her lovely fair skin and blue eyes but like my mother's previous fair child she was destined to pass away at an early age, about four years old. In 1899 I was born once more a child of my mother's colour like my sisters and then – joy of joys! – my mother gave birth to another son, again named Thomas, in December 1901. Later my younger sister Elizabeth was born; my mother adored her and this time she managed to keep her fair child.

In September 1902 I was taken ill with my throat. My mother attempted to cure the trouble by rubbing my neck gently with camphorated oil and winding round it a huge piece of flannel pinning it in position with a huge safety pin but when it did not improve Dr. Smith, then a comparatively young man, was called in. When he arrived he immediately, on looking into my throat, diagnosed that dreadful illness diphtheria. This was a great shock to my mother who had already buried two children for diptheria was a killer in those days.

While I was ill I remember very well lying in the little single bed at the foot of my mother and father's bed and hearing the men singing in the club room about seventy yards away. They used to have smoking concerts and the men would join in the chorus as the artists would sing their favourite songs. I remember that 'Blue Bell' and 'Dolly Grey' were two of their favourites and Emily would come and sit with her fingers in my ears to deaden the noise. She was my second eldest sister and always given the tasks which entailed responsibility.It was always she who would come and look through my hair to see if there were any 'dicky birds' hatched out in my fever and so enthusiastic did she become that I had bald patches on my poor little head, for she must, my mother said, always pull the nit from the hair, otherwise others would come along. So there could be no end to the never ending war on these horrible tantalizing little parasites who sucked their life from us in a most annoying and disgusting way. We could never neglect to do all in our power to keep them at bay by washing, combing and hunting them.

All my young life I can remember my mother working. When she had tidied the house, out would come the lace work. This method of swelling the family budget was carried out in most working class homes at the beginning of the century. The lace was taken from the factory to individual houses where the work was let out by the woman of the house to housewives for clearing. This entailed clipping all the surplus strands of cotton left on the lace so that the lovely patterns were thrown into relief. Sometimes the work would come in huge pieces which had to be separated. The work was poorly paid and my mother would sit for hours to earn a few shillings. While I was ill my mother would work late at night to pay the doctor and get the necessary medicines he prescribed but time went by and eventually I was allowed down stairs.

At this period one of the neighbours, Polly, would come and sit with my mother and the conversation would often become so animated that they both would forget I was there. Polly was about my mother's age. Her real name was Mary but apart from her husband no–one called her by her baptismal name. She had at this time five children all girls. One day I was sitting in the little scrubbed chair my father had made watching my mother's scissors fly over the surface of the lace she was clipping when Polly came in with her youngest child in her arms and seated herself on a stool facing my mother.

"She's been on all night again Becky, she's fairly wearing me out. When Nellie comes home I will send her to the chemist. A penn'orth of laudanum should do the trick," she said. "Laudanum, Polly! Surely not! You will ruin the poor little soul dull her wits, stupify her, make her dense. No, no. Try a sugar bar or one of those new fangled dummies the chemist sells, " answered my mother. But Polly would have none of this and insisted that a few drops on a bit of sugar never hurt any child.

I was still in the doctor's care and was not improving as I should. He suspected I had some parasite in my bowels and after many weeks I was sent to the General Hospital for a check. I remember the weekly visits very well. My mother brought me a dear little red cloak and hood to keep me warm for we had to walk a good half of the journey into town via Cut Through Lane and the rest we travlled on the tram car. The fare was one penny for an adult and one half penny for a child. We boarded the tram at the corner of Sherwin Road, Lenton and travelled along Castle Boulevard to the Fountain. From here we would walk up Stanford Street past the Castle Gate and on to Standard Hill, my mother telling me the history of the Castle and how the Luddites burned it down in the year 1831 and she never failed to remind me although I was so young that it was on Standard Hill that King Charles raised his standard.

I believe that I must have been one of the first patients to be x-rayed for I remember very plainly lying on a table in a dark room with a bright light over me. They located a huge tape-worm which, after treatment, eventually passed away in my motions. Being a very sensitive little girl the daily search was a great worry to me; I hated the proceedings but it had to be for the parasite had to be taken to the hospital carefully placed in a bottle of water for it was about six inches long. After many visits and dozens of bottles of Parish's Food and more Scott's Emulsion, not forgetting the interminable farthing's worth of peppermints which were kept in the dresser drawer and dished out with the medicine, I was eventually discharged from the hospital and our weekly trips were ended. My poor mother must have been pleased for, poor dear, what with her lace work and leaving my brother Tom with Polly, this journey must have worn her out for she was now about forty years of age and women aged quicker in those days for she, like many others had a hard life to keep us well fed and shod.

About this time I started School at Church Street, Beeston, and I loved it although I do remember that my very first day was marred by a bilious attack and to my great shame I was very sick at play-time under the shed where everyone could see me. There was a young pupil teacher in "The Babies", this was the name given to the first year children. We always called her Miss Lottie, I presume this was because her Christian name was Lottie. She must have been only seventeen years of age and because she was not a qualified teacher the older and more experienced women made this distinction and were more superior by adopting their surnames as titles. It was Miss Lottie who came along and comforted me. I loved her.

As time went on I was growing stronger, but was always a lean rather peeky little girl and my pale dark skin and big brown eyes did nothing to improve my appearance. I always looked so forlorn but despite my lack of good looks I was always liked and was developing into a clever little girl. My mother was delighted for despite the fact that she could neither read nor write herself she had a great desire that her children should benefit from the free education, now compulsory, and always sent us to school regularly. At this time many working class families failed to realise the value of going to school. The school attendance officer Mr. George Freeman who lived on Station Road would make his regular visits to the absentees. He always rode a three-wheeled cycle and we children always alluded to him as Daddy Freeman. To see his bearded figure sitting upright on his three-wheeler was enough to send any child hurrying off past the Town Hall and down Church Street to school. The only trouble I ever encountered was when I had to take the lace work back and could possibly be held up by the women as they chatted together forgetting I had to get back home with a fresh supply of work and then get to school on time, for punctuality was one of the things we were taught. I never remember being late although if I heard the school bell ringing I would hurry as fast as my legs could carry me. I could not run or put any strain on myself for the diphtheria I had suffered from left me with a weak heart and until I was seven years of age I was a very delicate child.

I loved the summer days when I was young although if the weather became too warm I would finish up with a bilious attack. My mother would bathe my head and before laying me on the sofa under the window in the only sitting room we had would put a vinegar cloth on my temples which would ease the throbbing considerably. Occasionally I would have a drink of lemon water which was always spoiled by a small amount of Epsom salts.

As well as the sitting room our house also had three bedrooms and an attic which had been used in previous times for the hosiery work which was carried on in the homes at that time, and a small kitchen where the coal was stored under the stairs. The stairs were not carpetted but were scrubbed with sand and soap every week. The dust from the coal underneath must have risen up through the cracks so how ever we kept those stairs so white I will never know.

We always had our Sunday dress which we wore when we went to the Sunday School classes and then it was put away along with our shoes until the following week. Those lovely days when the sun seemed to shine so brightly and if it did rain we would kneel on the sofa under the window and watch the heavy drops hit the ground and bounce off again. My mother would say "Watch the little men going to London" and this in my childish mind was what the rain drops looked like, hundreds of tiny men dashing along. Once when it was raining and blowing slightly my mother let me take my eldest sister's umbrella. I was just passing Acacia Walk when the wind suddenly blew a strong gust which caught the umbrella and blew it inside out. It really terrified me! Hanging on, I was blown for a few paces but in my childish mind I imagined I was going to be blown away and screamed my loudest. Someone took me home and my mother sent for a penny fairy story book and I never went to school that afternoon.

When my brother Tom started school despite my frailness I was always being called upon to help him in battles. Although he was of a rather quiet disposition, he was a big boy and the older boys thought he was older than he really was and he was often drawn into trouble. As a boy and long after, in fact until he joined the army at 17 years of age, he would always, on going to bed, stand on the second step of the stairs, turn round and address all in hearing – "Good night and God bless Mum. Good night and God bless Dad. And God bless everybody in the old wide world". He was a lovely boy. He had inherited my mother's lovely eyes and was very good looking.

At this time although people had little money they made great the family gatherings. The red letter days of our lives were the occasions when my Aunt Emma and Uncle Jack would visit us. Emma came from the mining town of Pinxton. After she married my uncle she was very good to my mother and it was from her home that she had married my father. My mother loved her brother dearly and together they used to sing the most lovely ballads for they both had good voices. Jack and Emma had no children but Aunt Emma was a gentle comely soul and we children were delighted when they came. We knew that there was a new penny for us all and at Christmas a small present.

At Christmas we always hung our stockings on a line across the mantlepiece and every one had a small present – an orange, an apple and perhaps a few sweets. My mother would always hang the kissing bush on the beam of the ceiling and how we loved to see the sugar mice and pigs hung there! The kissing bush was only a big bunch of evergreen and by the time twelfth night came along, when according to tradition all traces of Christmas festivities were removed, they along with the pigs, mice and paper garlands which festooned all the pictures were full of dust and smoke.

We always had a tall lamp on the middle of the table and my father would sit around making cork picture frames or drawing pictures of Ally Sloper who was a character in the comic paper "Ally Sloper's Half Holiday". There was a Sunday paper called "Illustrated Police Budget" with horrible illustrations of women in blazing night attire, their hair flying and the caption "Another Woman Burned to Death", or maybe the victims of this gruesome fate would be children. We were not supposed to see this paper but, as always, young ones have an uncanny delight in delving into forbidden territory. At other times my Dad would make shadow pictures with his hands. How we loved this! Then my mother, as she sat working on the lace, would read the pictures in the fire, but our greatest delight was to hear her sing.

I remember one nursery rhyme she used to teach us, one I have heard no-one else recite. It ran:–

There was a man and he went mad
and he ran up the steeple, and he cut off
the trail of his coat and threw it at the people.
There was a lady passing by
Who thought it rather funny,
She picked it up and wiped it dry
And sold it for some money.

The story of the poor man's predicament always made me feel very sad and I much preferred the stories of Hickory Dock or Sing a Song of Sixpence.

We were the leading country in the world and this, I believe, made up for a lot of misery. People suffered to help the country keep there. Wages were small and drunkenness was rife, children were neglected and poor, the old were ushered into the workhouses where most of them died. What could their children do? They had enough trouble bringing up their own children. Children died like flies most of them before reaching the age of one year. The sanitation was nil, and hygiene a thing only just beginning to be talked about. These were the good old days! In the towns beggars, cripples and the blind were just ignored, children ran about the streets barefoot in summer and winter. These conditions always made me very sad for I was, despite my bad temper at times, a very sensitive and feeling child as were all our family and although we had nothing to give away we were never in dire want like some poor souls. At this time lots of the houses were very old and were the abode of all kinds of parasites, cockroaches, fleas, bugs and mice which were to be found in most of them.

Religion was very popular – chapels, churches, Salvation Army halls were almost as numerous as the public houses. At this time they preached hell-fire and the old local preachers used to put the fear of God into me. Many times as a child I prayed that God would let me die before the end of the world for I dreaded being burnt up by the fire they told us about. I remember very clearly going to chapel one Sunday evening and the preacher, an old blood and thunder type – kept repeating in his sermon the words "Oh 'eavenly father, Oh 'eavenly father." When I reached home later my mother, as always, asked me what the preacher had told us and I answered "He kept telling us about Emily's father."

Voting day was a day to remember. From early morning until late in the evening the boys would parade the streets singing in praise of their particular parties and sending out derogatory parodies about their opponents. There were only two parties in those days – the blues and the yellow, Tory and Liberal. About a week before the day for their vote one such person came on a visit to our house. After informing my mother of the wonderful advantages she would have if her particular party was voted in, she prepared to leave with a persistant appeal, "Now Mrs. Martin, do your best to persuade your husband to vote for us, the advantages are great Mrs. Martin, you will never regret helping us into power Mrs. Martin, persevere Mrs. Martin," and my mother answered "Good Martin, good Martin" with great emphasis on the 'Martin'.

When I was about five, the Lockwoods came to live against us. They had two boys; the elder Harry was exactly my age and the younger one Willie was younger than my brother. All our childhood was spent in their company and Harry became my childhood sweetheart. He was always very kind to me and next to my own brother and sisters I loved him very much. In the summer when the days seemed so warm and sunny we would walk to Lenton Fields, where Nottingham University now stands, and gather all manner of flowers, lady smocks, cowslips, polly blobs, buttercups, daisies and the hedges were white over with May blossom. How lovely it was! We would walk down Humber Road until we came to Fletcher Road and then walk along by the Pasture Dyke where the flies and gnats would dance about the stagnant water and there would be a murmur of winged life. In spring the dyke was full of frog spawn and we would take along our jars to fill, taking them home and wait patiently until they turned into taddies. The Tottle Brook entered Lenton Fields here. After leaving Nottingham Road on very hot days we would paddle and sometimes, if we were very daring, walk right under the bridge to the other side. How quiet it was down there – the birds singing, the bees humming and an occasional clatter of the shunting of trucks on the sidings on the railway. There were very few motor cars at this time and the horse was still used for pulling carts, traps, tradesmen's vans and cabs. Life was very quite although I remember one day when one poor animal took fright and horse and cart came dashing down Stoney Street and straight into the shop window on the opposite side of the High Road. This caused great exitement.

We lived at number eight and next door were the Harpers. The father and mother were older than mine and they had three sons – George, Jack and Jim – all grown men. My mother always called Mrs. Harper 'Jenny' and occasionally when she alluded to her in her absence – 'Jenny Frizzle'. Jenny acquired this particular title by referring to her culinary art of frying as 'frizzling.' One morning early she chanced to meet my mother at the communal water tap which stood near our kitchen door. After a little chit-chat she suddenly turned away hastily with the words "Well I must hurry – I have to frizzle a bit of bacon for Jim's breakfast," – Jim being her husband – and the name of Jenny Frizzle stuck.

My mother had a great sense of humour. She gave all our neighbours nick-names. She always alluded to Mrs. Lockwood, a woman many years younger than herself, as Mrs. Featherbed. This was owing to Mrs. Lockwood trying to impress my mother with the fact that she and her husband Jack slept on a feather bed. Mr. Lockwood, he was always called 'Charley's Aunt' owing to the fact that every morning he would run past our house on his way to work – one could not fail to hear him as he wore clogs – and she would always say "There goes Charley's Aunt, still running." Mrs. Watkins, was known as Poverty Poll. This title was given her because she always told everyone that tale of how poor they were arousing people's pity and probably acquiring a few old clothes; her other name was Mrs. Leather Lips but I never knew why. Despite this particular trait of attaching titles to her neighbours, my mother was very well thought of and was a friend to many. If sickness struck any family they always sent for Mrs. Martin, although her tongue would lash them should the occasion arise. She could not and would not tolerate fools and let them know in no uncertain terms.

I can remember when Polly had a baby son named Frank after his father but he was a poor frail child and before reaching the age of one he passed away. Much was made of this and he was placed in an open coffin resting on two chairs for all and sundry to view. I shall never forget this sweet dear soul in his last bed. My sister Emily along with three other young girls of the same age carried him to his last resting place. Each girl wore a white dress with a broad black ribbon draped across the shoulder and tied with a bow on the hip. They made great splashes of these occasions and a tea would always follow the interment. On this particular day the refreshments were laid on but alas one of the mourners found a black beetle in the slab of currant cake laid out on the table. This caused great excitement everyone wanting to know from which particular shop it was bought and, although it was no unusual thing to find a beetle or fly in a loaf of bread or cakes, the speculation was great.

Over the wall from our back door was the yard of the pub further up the road and the landlord kept pigs. Although they were not near enough to be of any nuisance to us we could often hear the odd job man talking to them as he fed them or cleaned out the sty. He loved them and acquired the name of Billie Blessum because of his devotion to these very lowly animals. He was often to be seen walking along the High Road with a wooden contraption resting across his shoulders and from each end hung a hook on which would hang a bucket of swill which he would balance one each side. His trousers were caked with dried-on swill which had spilled over the sides of the buckets; he carried an appalling smell with him wherever he went with or without the buckets. One morning when taking the pigs their breakfast he met the butcher Thums who asked after the litter an old sow had just had and Billie immediately answered "They are doing nicely, blessum" – hence the name Billie Blessum. As a child I always thought this was his real name and was very surprised when I learned later that his surname was Thornhill. Once when we were sent with my elder sister Sarah Ann to get some rhubarb from our garden we had to go through the pub yard to get there, we had a look in the sty and Sarah Ann's straw sailor hat fell in among the pigs and to our consternation they gobbled it up. The band with the ship's name was devoured too, not a trace left, and we had to return home with the rhubarb but with one 6½d hat missing.

On Monday mornings the butchers' shops on the road would bring out their counters and chopping blocks on to the street and give them a scrubbing with soap and water. I loved to see the white soapy water flying about and when they had finished the job they would fling the rest of it left in the bucket on to the road. These were the days when the animals were driven from the Nottingham market all the way to Beeston by a cattle drover, then they were slaughtered locally and within an hour the carcasses would be seen hanging in the butchers' shops. I hated Wednesday afternoons for this was the day when on leaving school we would encounter the droves and the poor beasts about to meet their doom. Often they would run amok and people said the poor things could smell the slaughter house. Whether this was so I never truthfully knew, but I was always filled with great compassion for them, especially the sheep.

During my childhood there was a great patriotic feeling sweeping the country. We children were taught songs of our greatness in both military as well as naval power and our love of our country was second to none. Coming from a family where the father was an old soldier and the mother well trained in the love of her country and having two uncles who had fought in the Indian Mutiny, mother was a very patriotic person. She taught us to love our country always along with our love for our Maker. She would tell us of the disciplines practised in the Army at the time of the Mutiny. Both her uncles were in the Army but were in different divisions but once by a strange coincidence they met in India and celebrated by getting drunk. For this they were whipped in the presence of one another – such was the hard life of a soldier in those times.

I remember well seeing the first aeroplane to fly over Beeston. What an awe-inspiring sight – so fragile – it looked like thin laths of wood nailed together, yet there it was sailing through the sky so effortlessly. We had previously seen the balloons up there but this was something so different we could scarcely believe our eyes. My mother stood silently as we watched when the plane and its occupant pass overhead then very quietly she turned to my sisters and myself and said "My, my! What will England come to?" If someone had told her that before many years England was to lose her power as the master of the world, she would have called him traitor so steeped was she in love for her country and the Royal family.

My mother and my father were two extremes in looks as well as temperament, she being exceedingly dark with luminous brown eyes and high cheek bones with her very soft dark hair growing in little tendrils on the back of her neck. She was very small of stature, about five foot one inch in height and very pleasing to look at. She certainly had a determined and definite mind but despite this she was most lovable. On the other hand, my father – a good-looking man with sandy coloured hair and very blue eyes – was a man who needed a lot of leading. He was a peace-loving and very tender-hearted man. His face would work in distress as he would try to keep back the tears if he heard of anything that touched his heart strings. We had toys, most of which he had made – a horse with a lovely mane painted with white and black paint, dappled effect; a grand push-cart painted with red and white, the long handles made from broom sticks and the fancy wood work nothing but clothes pegs split in half and placed round the body to form a pattern. He would always mend our shoes and many times I have been sent for a piece of leather and a half-penny worth of sprigs to mend one of the children's footwear. The baby chair with the hole in the seat was made by him and he even made a huge strong fire-guard that went all round the kitchen fire. In cold weather he would always sit on this contraption and warm his hind quarters before retiring.

Despite the fact that my father was a tender hearted man who had a steady job and was a hard worker, like the majority of the males of this period he was a very irresponsible man, selfish and thoughtless. And he had one important failing – he drank. When he was in drink he was a different man entirely from the one who had been in the home for the rest of the week although he was not disagreeable when under the influence of drink as were many other men of the time. His greatest downfall was being the possessor of two medals received for service in the war with the Mahdis. These medals were the pride of my mother's life but were the source of all my father's troubles. He could pawn them along with the waistcoat they were pinned on for the princely sum of two shillings and sixpence and this, when the spirit moved him, was what he would do. Should he get the urge to have a Monday from work he would steal them out and go along to Daddy Wilson's where Uncle John would lend him one bright half-crown on them, but they were always redeemed on Saturday dinner-time ready for financing another of his escapades.

He was not by himself, for most of the manual workers of this period indulged in these self-administered holidays, known as Saint Mondays, and little wonder for they were little more than slaves and a man must show his authority in some way even if his family suffers for his privilege. Unless unduly aroused my father was never a violent man as were some of the men of this time. In fact I used to wonder if he had loved Polly Perkins very much for he would always sing this particular ditty stressing the fact that *"She was as beautiful as a butterfly and proud as a queen, his pretty Polly Perkins from Paddington Green".* Despite his faults he was an excellent worker being head furnace man at Beeston Foundry for thirty-six years. He was riddled with spark burns all over his body and not a hair was on his arms. It was exceedingly hard work – no wonder he broke out at times. Often my mother would tell me especially on Monday mornings to go and look in the black box to see if my father's waistcoat was there; he always laid it on the top of his trousers and pinned on the left breast were his medals from the Egyptian war. If he was thinking of having a day off, the waistcoat would be gone and she knew she would be a day's money short the following Saturday.

This was in the days when the pubs were open all day and she, poor woman, would work all the harder at the lace to help make up what she would be short at the end of the week. When she said "Now children be very quiet; your dad is lying down." we knew why although she never said a word against him to us children or allowed anyone else to speak against him. Despite his way of life I believe he loved my mother very much and she adored him although there were times when she would give him a length of her tongue. In his sober days he wouldn't even answer, he was a naturally quiet man, but if the drink was in him he would retaliate but there was never any animosity after.

My mother was a very strong character and she hardly had to speak – a glance was enough – her mouth would set firm and the eyes would flash the message and we children would never think of answering or defying her. But her love was abundant and she would caress and love you in such a sweet manner; one child was no more to her than another although because I was such a frail child, she was always especially mindful of me. As a family we were very close and this is how she tried to bring us up to cling to one another. She spilled over her love, always fair and understanding.

By the time I was seven I began to get stronger but still far from robust and my brother was now as tall as I was. I progressed at school and by the time I was nine I was very good at English and excelled in essays. I was awarded a certificate for one of the best on the subject "Prevention of cruelty to dumb animals". I was very proud of this and so was my mother. She showed everyone my reports – the bread-man Mr. Gore, the insurance man, the doctor, in fact anyone she could get interested in my wonderful ability to come, if not top, very near this position. What a wonderful woman she was! I loved to please her and because I knew how pleased she would be with my efforts I worked all the harder. But sewing I could never do well. I always set off with my little piece of linen in such a confident manner but before I had gone very far with the hemming it always seemed somehow to get soiled and tatty with my little hot hands. I knew this and it always caused me great worry for I wanted very badly to get good marks to please my mother. She was my inspiration.

My mother was never very well after the birth of our youngest sister. She would have fainting bouts and later as she became ill her skin took on a yellow look. No-one took much notice of this, least of all myself for I was only nine years old and things seemed, after she had recovered from one of these attacks, to go on exactly as they always had. She would sit at the lace work just the same as always and sing and talk to us in the evenings in the manner we had always been used to. Although she would stay up late at night in order to have the lace ready to return before we children went to school, she would always see we younger ones were in bed at a reasonable time. She would without fail sing us a lullaby and counsel us to be good children and not forget to say our prayers. A candle was placed at the end of the long passage which divided the bedrooms and this would give enough light to both rooms and help dispel any fears we had of bogey men, black men or even ghosts we imagined lingered in dark places. There was always one night in the week when we would be awakened from our slumbers by the rough whispering voices of men and then perhaps would follow a hurried bang and the distant rumble. This never really upset us for we knew these midnight marauders to be what was known as the night soil men or as some less polite folks would call them 'The Muck Majors'. We knew when that particular delight was drawing near by the amount of refuse in the lavatory tub. By the time the cart and men arrived things had begun to get a little chaotic in the small house at the end of the yard.

Every evening the boiler that sat on one side of the fire-place (the oven was on the other) had to be filled to the top to ensure hot water for our morning wash and other household work. Woe betide the family if the boiler ever happened to run low for my father always insisted on plenty of water and soap for health's sake, and was not cleanliness next to Godliness, although at this time there was a profusion of unclean ungodly mortals walking about, Gold help them!

Eventually mother's illness got worse, the doctor was sent for and she was rushed off to the General Hospital. I shall never forget that Saturday morning in September 1909. I was ten years of age.

It was my job on Saturday mornings to deliver the garden produce which Jenny next door sold. Mr. Harper and his sons were excellent gardeners and had allotments at both the Bog and the Drop gardens and they always had plenty of customers for the harvest of their labours. My sister Emily used to do the job of delivering orders until she started work at 13 and then I took it over. I had returned from delivering an order and Jenny, Mrs. Harper, said to me "Lottie, your mother would like to see you." Knowing my mother was ill and in bed I wondered what she could want me for. But on going outside there was a cab waiting at our house and again I wondered why this should be there. Polly was just wrapping blankets around my mother and I noticed she still had her nightdress on. My poor dear loving sensible and martyred mother, the one who always gave us all such good advice, who kissed us when we were poorly and smacked us when we were naughty, how ill she looked. I cried. She turned to me and said "Lottie, always be a good girl. Look after your brother and sister and do what Emily tells you." As a rule she would say "Do what your older sisters say" but my sister Sarah Ann was ill too and lying in the back bedroom. She was to follow my mother into hospital in less than a week with typhoid fever and this was the reason she alluded to Emily. I never saw my mother alive again.

I knew she was very ill for my father and Emily would go to the hospital at such peculiar times, once in the middle of the night, and in my childish mind I knew that this was not the usual procedure. Being an out-patient of the hospital when I was younger, I knew that there were specified hours when one visited the patient, so it was no surprise when the policeman called at the house this particular morning.

Emily and my father had gone to the hospital early in the morning and I was left to get Tom my brother off to school and to look after Lizzie. A knock came to the door and there stood a policeman; he asked for my father and I told him he had gone to the hospital with my sister. I fetched Polly and he must have told her my mother had passed away for she came straight into the house and drew all the blinds. Never let any one draw the blinds when I am gone; this action filled me with horror, to shut out the light to plunge us into gloom was almost more than I could bear. I knew my mother was dead, that I would never hear her voice again. How sad and unhappy I was! The blinds were not opened again until the following Monday when we buried her.

The Monday morning of the funeral was a lovely dry sunny September morn; I shall always remember it. My sister Emily was very busy making all last minute arrangements. There were mine and Lizzie's little black dresses to fetch from a neighbour who had kindly offered to make them, and I was sent to the haberdashery shop for three pairs of white gloves, one pair ladies, two pairs childrens and four black edged handkerchiefs, one gents, three ladies. What a sad procession we made my father and Emily with Lizzie in the middle and my brother Tom and myself behind them and other relations to follow! It was the first time I had ever been in a cab and I shall never forget the horrible fusty smell when the steps were taken up and the door closed; I felt I would vomit. But the worst moment was to come, I did not mind particularly when the coffin was lowered into the grave, but when the minister reached that part of the service when he said ashes to ashes, dust to dust, my poor little heart felt broken as the earth he had taken into his hand was dropped with a dull thud on the coffin lid. I knew that very soon they would be putting spades full of soil on, and eventually the whole grave would be filled in and I would see my darling mother no more. There would be no more singing while she chipped away at the lace, in fact, the last work she had was returning to the house from where it was distributed to the willing hands waiting for their individual quota.

Sarah Ann was still in the hospital, but Emily who was at this time about 17½ years old, took over the running of the house and took care of the younger children myself 10, Tom 7 and Liz 4 and in some ways life seemed, for a few weeks at least, to become easier. As there was no lace to take back or collect I could go about my young life in a much more leisurely way particularly in the morning.

Our neighbours were a great consolation after mother died. I was always a great favourite with the Harpers and I would often sit by their fire. Now that mother was gone we never heard Mrs. Harper alluded to as Jenny Frizzle and we would not be so presumptuous as to take on the familiarity of using the title for we were only children so henceforth she was always given her correct name. How I loved to read the comic papers like 'Chips' and 'Comic Cuts' her sons always had an abundance of with their beloved characters Butter Ball, Weary Willie, Trowsey Triddle and Casey Court.

On Friday Mrs. Harper would always make home-made beer and I was sent for the balm to set this concoction working. I used to take a huge blue mug for a pennyworth of balm from the 'Greyhound' public house on the High Road where they brewed their own beer at this time. The landlord Sid would say "Go down the cellar to George; he will give it to you" and down I would go each step wet and clingy with continual usage and at the bottom large tubs of beer working and bubbling over with balm on the top of each. What a lovely sight! The creamy rich thick concoction moving in rhythm! I loved to see it and when the mug skimmed along the top of the vat I envied George the operation. Along with a most salubrious smell and the hope that the brewer would leave a little balm clinging on the mug which I would immediately lick off, I think fetching the penn'orth of balm was one of the tasks I loved most. When Saturday night came along Mrs. Harper's herb beer was ready in bottles for her clients and in the summer Sunday dinner was never complete without a glass to wash down the young ones' meal. Older people at this time would have a jug of ale.

Although the neighbours were a help to we motherless children we missed our darling mother very much. I think it was her love that left such a void for despite what happened she was always there with her love and counsel. No-one could replace the love, not for me nor, I think, for my father. I believe he missed her very much when she died. He never married again although he lived for sixteen years after. He was sixty-four when he passed away and is buried in the same grave as my mother in Beeston cemetry along with the little girl Lily.

Although father was still with us it was mostly thanks to the combined efforts of my two elder sisters that we were brought up as our dear mother would have wished. It was a confounding task for those so young but by the grace of God they managed. But for me, I knew in my childish mind that I had lost the person who gave me all the love, encouragement and understanding I needed and that henceforth I was to fight a lone fight.

Chapter 2 GROWING UP 1909 – 1919

As I look back I think 1909 must have been the beginning of change for ordinary people. In January of that year the Old Age Pension came into operation; all persons over the age of 70 years were entitled to this benefit. It was a wonderful step forward. Previously a person had to be very nearly destitute to be able to apply to the local council for help, and then relief was only given if they had no children in a position to help. Often the younger people would help their parents, to the detriment of their own families or because of the disgrace everyone attached to receiving relief. Old people had, prior to 1909, to become paupers for owing to years of previous deprivation their health and energy failed long before the reached three score years and ten. I remember going to Dr. Smith's surgery most Fridays to collect the medicine for Granny Mellors who lived with her son and daughter at No. 6. Donna was her daughter and Jack her husband was brother to Mr. Harper who lived at No. 10. Hence two Harpers lived very close to each other. Granny was a dear old soul, she always smoked a clay pipe, as did quite a few of the very old ladies of this time and she would often send me for a penn'orth of laudanum to help make her sleep. She also loved chlorodine and liquorice tablets. These, she said, were for her bronchitis. When she died I remember being very much afraid, not because of the old lady who was always a dear, but from awe as I could not reconcile myself to the doctrine of when we passed away we immediately either went to heaven or hell. Strange I never felt any fear when my mother passed away, perhaps because having died in hospital she was never put on show as most of the corpses of this period were. Neighbours, relations, friends and hangers on would parade in front of the coffin which was kept open until the hour of its removal to the cemetery. They were a gruesome lot and there was always great competition as to who could put on the most elaborate funeral. If they were old with no family the old person was buried by the Parish, this was a great stigma. But Granny Mellors as we always called her was buried in great style and quite in order.

Should a person become incapacitated or unable to work, he could not apply for the pension until he had reached 70 years of age and most of the old people lived in dire want for many were too proud to apply for Parish help and only had the few shillings from their children and a little food from their neighbours. There was always some generous soul who would help keep the spectre of starvation away, a lump of coal from one, a candle or two or even a meal would be offered. But not all old people were lucky enough to have kind people around them and invariably these products of a world that worked them hard for small wages, ended their days at Basford Workhouse, to die the death of a pauper. But times were changing and the pension of 5/– was more than acceptable to all the old who lived to receive it.

It was about this time that Jane Harper reached the age of seventy. This I knew because one morning on my way to school she called me into her comfortable kitchen and asked if I would do something for her that she wanted keeping a secret. Intrigued by such a request I went immediately after my dinner to her house all agog to know what this mysterious request was. On the table under the window on which was always a red tablecloth stood a bottle of Blue Black Ink, a pen and a small document. This she requested me to read, which of course I did for she herself could neither read nor write, since like many of her contemporaries she had never had any schooling. It was from the Ministry of Pensions requesting her to fill in all the particulars needed. Every detail was filled in and the papers placed in the addressed envelope supplied. Then came the solemn moment when almost on her knees she begged of me to tell no-one, not even Sarah Ann. Poor old soul! She thought it was accepting charity and wanted no one to know she was about to receive the Old Age Pension. Needless to say I never told anyone at all until years later when she had passed on.

Goose Fair 1909 arrived, we loved this, not because of the roundabouts or games, because often we would never see the fair, but always we would have a present known as a fairing. Liz and I would invariably have a doll, straw body and wax face with such lovely blue eyes and straw coloured hair; Tom would have a drum or bugle.

The fair was held about a fortnight after my mother's death. It was always held at the beginning of October for three days. My sister Sarah Ann had not yet left hospital and Emily was still at home with us so it was decided that she would take us to the fair.

It was Friday morning the first week in October that we all set out accompanied by Katie Watkins, one of Polly's children. We must have looked a pathetic little party in our deep mourning dress and sixpence between us to pay the tram car fare from Sherwin Road to the market place and the return ride, but Katie had two pence all to herself.

We set off along the High Road and what was then called Nottingham Road until we crossed the Tottle Brook bridge and into Cut Through Lane. This beautiful country lane has now been swallowed up by the Nottingham University, but we were not to know this at that time, and revelled in the quiet beauty of our journey into town.

The approach to the lane was lovely in itself for the huge trees on either side of the road were turning on their autumn colours of gold and bronze, but when one entered the lane everything became a veritable fairy land.

The squirrels were beginning to fill their store houses with nuts from the beech and were so daring we wondered if they could see us. On the right side of the narrow lane ran a very small trickle of clear water and the birds were bathing and flapping their wings in their morning ablutions. The path slowly wound its way up-hill and on reaching the top one could see quite a large part of the city. The castle and Colwick Woods were plainly visible. A lovely beech tree stood here over on the left and the fallen nuts lay on the ground in profusion. Going down the hill and to the right were what was known as the Hollows and the rabbits would hold their frolicks here in the cool autumn evenings. In the distance could be heard the shunting of the engines on the sidings at Lenton. The dull thud of the meeting of the buffers made a sound like drums in the great orchestra of the music made by the birds and an occasional moo from the cattle grazing in the Hollows added to the accompaniment. Running down hill we were soon at the junction of Cut Through Lane, Spring Close and Sandy Lane which ran from Dunkirk up to Derby Road.

The Derby Road side was nothing more than a one-man track, the sand lying heaped on both sides. It is hard to believe that Clifton Boulevard – that wide dual road with a flyover at one end and a huge traffic control at the north – now runs on this very lane.

So we pressed on through Spring Close and over the canal bridge, by the Tan Works, that evil smelling factory, which supplied work for a big proportion of the local inhabitants who lived on Leen Side, past the white-washed cottages on to Gregory Street with its quaint quiet surroundings on past the Church to Sherwin Road Schools where we mounted the tram on our last stage of the journey to Nottingham Goose Fair 1909. The fair – that wonderful conglomoration of roundabouts, boxing booths, candy and rock stall, ginger snaps and Grantham ginger bread stalls, not forgetting the menagerie, Bostock and Womballs and best yes, best of all, the side shows the largest being Collins'. There was always a free show on the front to entice the would-be audience inside, and we quickly took up our positions at the front of the Exchange Buildings, standing Lizzie on the windowsill of the Public House in order that she would be able to see the free show. This was the year Peary had reached the North Pole and the dancing girls were dressed as Eskimos. How wonderful we thought this to be, but alas when the girls disappeared from the scene and the public were clamouring to reach the pay box in order to see more of these wonderful exotic creatures who were enticing them into the interior of the tent for further entertainment, we had to press on.

Beecrofts that wonderful emporium of toys stood on the corner of the Exchange Buildings and dolls of every size and description were hanging outside the doors. Huge strawfilled bodies with wax faces, blue eyes and golden hair, and smaller dolls with kid bodies some jointed and, wonder of wonders, some even went to sleep. For the boys engines and perhaps a car, for this form of travel was slowly taking over, but up to now the horse was still very much in favour.

Carried by the crowd we found ourselves in the centre of the fair and Katie had brought a lovely blue necklace from one of the vendors who was displaying his wares on a pole, one penny each string. "Choose your own colour." How I envied her! The stalls were right up The Poultry and Smithy Row even up Queen Street. Coconuts, pot peas etc.

We made our way home using the tram cars which rumbled along Castle Boulevard past the Castle Rock and on to Sherwin Road from where we had to leg it, Emily holding Lizzie's hand encouraging her along. I was glad to leave the tram, the jolting made me feel sick and reminded me of a journey I had once taken with my father and mother when I was younger. On this occasion we were travelling along Woodborough Road to Mapperley Hospital when everything went black. The tram was stopped and we alighted and I was sat on a wall to rest while my elders tried to revive me. I never liked tram cars after this experience.

The evening was drawing in by the time we reached the Lane but we stopped to scoop up the beech nuts still lying at the top of the hill under the tree. The air was filled with sweet scents and noises of nature preparing for sleep when Shipstone's clock struck the hour of seven. We had nothing as a momento except the beech nuts which we planned to transform into necklaces and bracelets which even Katie's blue beads would not equal, or so we thought. Alas, like Katie's baubles, the trinkets did not last long. The thread we strung them on was too thin, but what joy as we placed the small fruits of that lovely tree upon the table and by the light of the oil lamp made our individual effort to see who would thread the most and have the longest necklace.

It was about a fortnight after our trip to the fair that Sarah Ann came home from hospital after her long and severe illness and took over from Emily in the House. Emily went back to her work at the Tan works at Lenton, hard, dirty, smelly but well paid compared with those in the lace factories and at the Telephone works. Emily excelled at her work and the boss always alluded to her as 'Lightning' because of her speed.

Sarah Ann was a very nice looking young woman, dark hair which hung around her like a huge black velvet cap when it was not pinned up on her head in a roll, the fashion of the moment. Her dark luminous eyes were set in an oval face, her complexion was creamy white with very little colour; many said she had the features of a Madonna. But although she loved children very much she treated our dad very poorly; I always thought she blamed him for the death of mother. A battle of supremacy was going on between father and daughter, Sarah Ann letting it be plainly seen that she was not going to submit in any way. Agreed, he could be aggravating to the point of almost despair and on the occasions when the medals were left in the safe keeping of 'Uncle' the situation was worsened for we all knew that this could entail not only a day from work but may be a week —this with no wages. There was little wonder that we all developed an inferiority complex for being of a proud nature inherited from our mother we tried in every way, as she had done, to cover up for him.

It was quite a while before Sarah Ann mastered him. He stood up to her but when she married Ern he gradually came under the hammer. I remember quite well one of the fights he put up. She had been saving for a chamber set for her bottom drawer. This comprised of wash bowl and jug, soap dish sponge jug and two chambers all decorated with a lovely floral pattern of roses. This lovely array of room furnishing had recently been acquired and duly stored but on this particular Saturday evening something went wrong, probably a row about money, I never really knew. What I do know was that suddenly we young ones were whisked over to the Watkins' house and Sarah Ann's toilet set was placed outside the door for all and sundry to view; we were turned out. Poor old dad! Of course we all poled back the very next morning to get our Sunday clothes in preparation for Sunday school, and life resumed its usual course. I believe this was one of the last stands he made although he would attack her from behind his closed bedroom door often using unprintable language in so doing.

Despite all this we all had a great sense of humour and could laugh at ourselves when we were alone together but never with others for we never discussed anything about our intimate life – this would have been thought too degrading. On one particular Saturday afternoon when Dad had retired for his siesta, which he always did on Saturday and Sunday after dinner, Emily had occasion to go upstairs for some reason. After quietly creeping down to the living room again in a voice quiet and subdued she said in an almost theatrical manner "Children be as quiet as little mice. Your Dad is asleep and snoring like a pig. Could you belong to the farm yard?" Her appeal for silence was accepted but it was only after a great effort that we refrained from laughing – we could all see the funny side of the situation.

Despite all Dad's faults we loved him, even Sarah Ann would, in her more tolerant moments, make excuses for him, which, by the way, were not often.

About this time Sarah Ann would go to help Mrs. Hemming the chemist's wife on the High Road working several hours a day for the exorbitant wage of half a crown but this small sum helped to swell the family finances – a lot could be done with half a crown. Mrs. Hemming was more of adviser and friend but like the rest of people was ready to exploit you. Even at this tender age I was an expert pastry hand and Sarah Ann full of praise for my handiwork told Mrs. Hemming and she immediately asked for my services on Saturday mornings to make her mince pies. This I had to do in between delivering the green groceries for Mrs. Harper. I was always terrified that the poor old dear would enquire where I had been so long but I never remember her doing so. Needless to say the pastry-making must have

2. The Cross, Beeston c. 1900

3. Silver Hill, Nottingham Road, Beeston c. 1912

4. The Square and Monument, Beeston c. 1905

5. High Road, Beeston c. 1914

6. Chilwell Road, Beeston 1920s

7. "The fire brigade was called... the engine was drawn to the alarming scene by two stalwart horses"(p.28) **Beeston Fire Brigade 1920s**

8. "I used to take a huge blue mug for a pennyworth of balm from the Greyhound public house" (p.16) **Greyhound Inn, Beeston High Road 1929**

9. "The motor car was gradually taking over from the horse-drawn carriage and Thomas Barton of Chilwell had about two charabancs on the road."(p.32) **Barton Charabanc - operated on the Beeston to Nottingham service 1916-21**

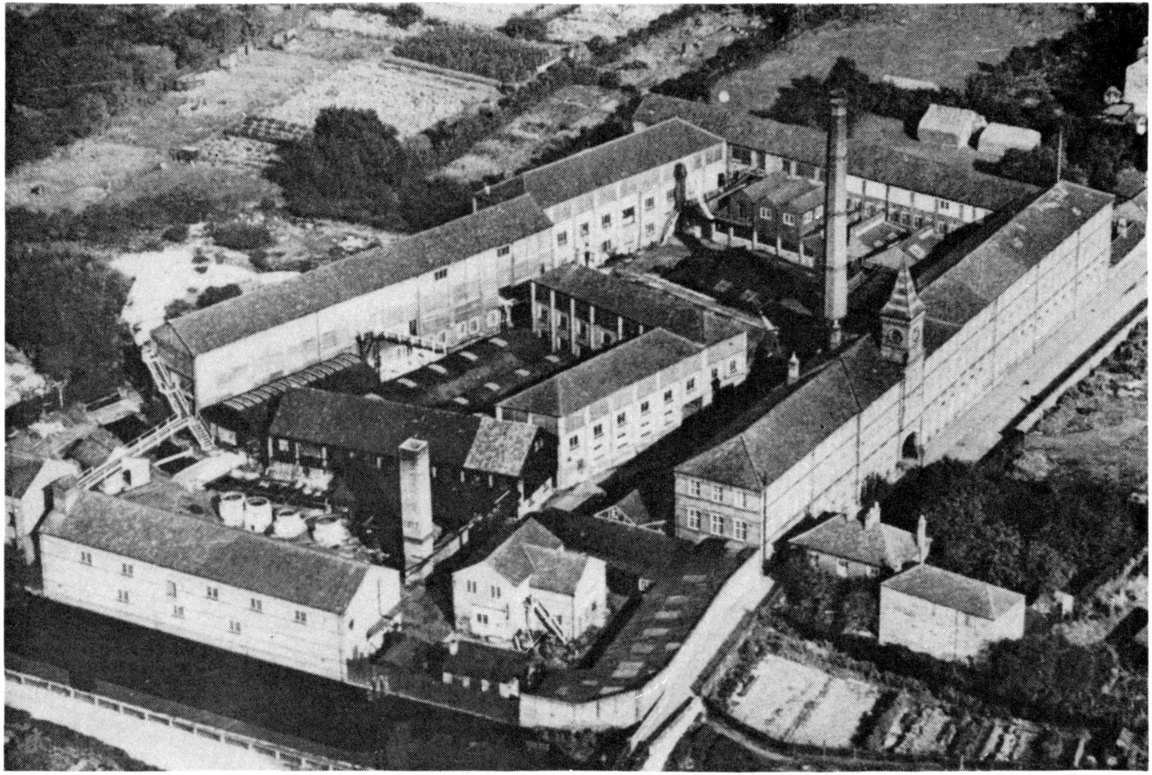

10. "This awful place..." where Lottie learned" the mysteries of the processing of animal skins into leather" (p.30) **Bayley's Tanning Yard, Lenton**

11. "This beautiful country lane...when one entered everything became a veritable fairyland" (p.19) **Cut Through Lane c. 1905**

12. "We boarded the tram at the corner of Sherwin Road, Lenton and travelled along Castle boulevard to the Fountain" (p.5) **Trams at the Walter Fountain, Nottingham c. 1904**

13. "Beecrofts - that wonderful emporium of toys" (p.20) **Beecrofts Toy Shop, Nottingham 1900s**

14. "That wonderful conglomeration of roundabouts, boxing booths, candy and rock stalls and Grantham gingerbread stalls" (p.20) **Goose Fair 1909**

15. "....and best of all, the side shows, the largest being Collins" (p.20) **Goose Fair 1908**

16. "Queen Mary and King George the Fifth made a visit to Nottingham....It was a glorious day!" (p.34) **Nottingham June 1914**

17. "Poor lads they had no idea what they were going to...." (p.34) **Troops On Trent Bridge - The Day Before The War Began 1914**

18. "We waved them all off on their adventure with the song **Farewell Isabelle**" (p.35)

19. "We were to be trained to drive the overhead cranes which were suspended on rails on the roof of the building" (p.35) **Girls on Cranes at Chilwell Factory c. 1916**

20. "In December 1916 the factory was visited by King George V" **Chilwell Factory 1916**

been considered a labour of love for I never remember receiving any compensation for stealing the time from my other employer.

School was still the place, apart from home, that I loved the best and it was always my ambition to work hard and become a teacher. Now no-one at home encouraged me except perhaps in my cooking but I loved the praise and attention I got at school. I loved my work and my teachers were always so kind to me not because I was dressed well or indeed looked well for I was never considered a pretty child – quite the reverse in my estimation – but I spoke very well and was never rowdy or ill-behaved to them and I know that they appreciated the fact that I tried very hard so one or the other would at times praise me. I was still progressing at school and I was never lower in class than the third from top. Don't think I had no competition, for I had. Several of the girls had good tutors at home – the Reverend Homer's daughter Gladys, and Doris Hemsley, whose mother taught at the school, along with the Atkinson's girls and Margery Downs whose father was a well educated man.

Life went on much the same until Sarah Ann informed us that she was going to return to her work at the Tan factory and she trusted us to all co-operate to make the financial situation easier. We all agreed to be very good children and help. My duties were to see that Liz and Tom went to school in the manner to which we had been accustomed, brush Liz's hair, see that Tom always pulled up his stockings which boys as well as girls wore at this time and peel the potatoes ready for Mrs. Watkins to boil for our dinner. The stew or broth was always left in the oven which was always warm.

This was the procedure for about a year until the Watkins family went to Paisley in Scotland, Mr. Watkins having lost his work along with many others when the Humber Cycle Works had closed down and gone to Coventry. This caused a lot of hardship in Beeston, remember there was no dole in those days only the parish relief and people were literally starving, hence the departure of the Watkins for fresh pastures. We all went to the station that Friday night to wish them a good journey and luck when they arrived for they had been good friends to us. After their departure life was just that little harder for us children but Polly despite her moaning ways had always been there, like the day when Tom was nearly drowned in the dyke on Dovecote Lane.

Along with Harry and Willis Lockwood we had been to the recreation ground which had recently been opened, Louis Pearson having given the council a present of the site. On our way back home the boys were attracted by the running dyke and decided to walk across by clinging to the wooden barrier, alas when Tom reached the middle the structure gave way and let him fall face downwards into the murky water. After some struggling Harry and I managed to pull him out, but not before he had almost filled his lungs. As luck would have it we laid him on the grass verge on his side; this action save his life for he pumped up the water from his innards like a fountain and soon regained conciousness. This was fate taking a hand if you like, for we children knew nothing of artificial respiration. In fact I doubt if we had ever heard of it. We took off his clothes and wrapped my pinafore around him and were not long in returning home. Polly said to get him in a hot bath and all would be well. Now we were all assembled to see these very good friends on their journey.

Sarah Ann was always interested in religion and always saw that we went to Sunday School and Chapel. About this time the Gospel Mission was visited by an Evangelist, Robert Reith he drew the crowds by his beautiful singing voice, he was known as the Singing Evangelist. I was always afraid of the Hell Fire religion some of the local preachers handed us, and he was no exception, but when he sang he enthralled me. I loved to join in and always imagined that my mother was in heaven and could hear me.

Eventually I began to wonder how this could possibly be, was she not in the grave, I saw them put her there so how could she possibly be up in the sky clothed in white singing hymns along with the heavenly choir? The situation worried me a lot although I had often been told that when we died we went to live with the angels but who were these angels? They must have been complete strangers to my mother. Was she happy with them as everyone seemed to think the dead were? I could not decide. Surely she did not like them better than her own little children? Did she sing to them as she used to us? I could not make up my mind – but decided to be on the safe side and went to the penitent John trembling and full of apprehension. Perhaps I would now understand why my mother had died and left us all but I never did.

When Sarah Ann decided that she was going to be baptised we were all very impressed. I remember going to the Union Church on Dovecote Lane for the ceremony. There were several young men and women about to participate in the ceremony. The organ and congregation were singing "Jerusalem the Golden" when they filed in, the women in white gowns with their hair flowing. Sarah Ann looked so angelic, her hair hanging around her like a huge cape. Each one walked into the water and after the necessary words were chanted the officiating minister emersed each one underneath. I never knew what effect this had on her, for she never said, but personally I never saw any difference in her at all.

The Beeston Town Band was much in evidence around at this time and they would play for all local functions including the Wakes Parade and the Flower Show held on the Dovecote Lane Recreation ground when gardeners all and sundry competed for prizes, the proceeds going to the Nottingham General Hospital. But these occasions made very little impression on my musical tastes. I remember more the awe inspired feeling I had when the band paraded the High Road on the death of

Edward the Seventh and again at the sinking of the Titannic when of course the awesome melancholy Dead March in Saul was played.

I can also remember very plainly hearing the Dead March played at the funeral of a veteran of the Crimean War whose name was Oldham. He was carried on a gun carriage from Willoughby Street to Beeston Cemetery with full military honours, the band playing the Dead March all the way. This music always made me wonder why if we went to heaven immediately at death people were so sad about it. Was this occasion not a time for being happy that our dear ones were now safe from the cares and worries of this sad world? Did we go to heaven as the preachers would have us believe or were we in that cold place I had seen allocated to my dear mother? By this time I was learning many things but no-one had yet been willing to enter into any conversation concerning where we were all going and why.

I would often wonder why life was so unfair to some. Being the eldest of the three young ones I was held responsible for most things that happened. If some boy gave Tom a licking, why was I not there to prevent it? Or if Tom showed his authority over Liz by giving her a punch why did I not stop him? If Liz or Tom fell into the hands of any little hooligans I was always blamed for not being on the scene at that particular moment and helping to avoid the catastrophe. I always tried to do right to my younger brother and sister but I was always blamed if anything went wrong and this hurt me terribly for I was alluded to as a bad girl which did not improve my outlook and caused me to become aggressive. No wonder I became pugnacious for I was always on the alert for all situations.

I remember plainly one terrible occasion when I was dubbed 'That bad girl'. It was one summer's day when we and the Lockwood boys were playing on the gardens, a couple of plots of land which were not cultivated by the tenant of a house on the yard. Every tenant had a garden but in this particular case the householder was a man with one leg and one arm who we always called the Peggy-leg man. He was a shoe repairer, and a good one at that, but he could not dig his garden, hence the lovely play-ground we always had at the extreme end of the yard away from the houses and traffic of the High Road. At the bottom end of the garden stood a plum tree whose trunk yielded a sticky glue substance which we delighted in removing along with the plums. It was on one such occasion that we were playing house and Harry took a tin kettle we had acquired and claimed it was his own. Immediately I gave chase, caught him by the sleeve of which I would not let go and eventually out came the sleeve allowing him to fall on a piece of glass lying amongst the grass. He had three stitches put in his hand. Imagine my feelings! That bad girl again!

I also have cause to remember another occasion when the whole family was angry with me. That particular Sunday afternoon we were to be taken to have our pictures done at the amateur photographers. Liz and Tom were really lovely children but I was as plain as plain could be, rather lean, not thin but lean, with a peaky face, huge dark eyes and an olive-looking skin with a rather pronounced forehead made to look more prominent by my hair always being drawn very tightly into a knot on the top of my head. I used to have severe headaches but I never dared loosen my hair in case I was called an untidy child. On this occasion I did so want my hair dressing in the same way as Liz with a bow of ribbon on each side but Sarah Ann was adamant about it and said "No. Only one bow for you." I wondered why – did not Liz always look nicer than I? She had prettier hair and face than myself – why should Sarah Ann give her more than me? This was the thought I voiced and for my cheek I was given a smart tap across the face. Of course she first had to catch me and this inflamed her more.

As usual Sarah Ann had hold of Liz by one hand and Tom by the other, myself walking behind with a strict order of not to loiter. This little procession set off up Chilwell Road for Mr. Wormall's house – he lived at the top of Hall Croft. While we were en route I decided to spoil the picture, little knowing that I was only spoiling it for myself, for I have always had to live with it since. There was Sarah Ann seated with Tom and Liz at her side smiling like little angels and I, a little to the side, with a sad and sulky face. I was never a beauty but this photograph made me, if anything, plainer looking than I was. Woe is me!

Although I was thought of as a bad girl at home, at school and with the neighbours I was considered a well-spoken, intelligent child. I was still progressing at school and sat examinations with a view to further education when I reached the age of thirteen but alas this was not to be. Apart from the fact that I would have to buy, or Sarah Ann would have to buy, my uniform and books and pay my train fare every day to Nottingham, she had other ideas for me. I never reached Brincliffe College and my ideas of becoming a teacher like Miss Lottie never materialized.

I left school the day I was thirteen and was told that now I was to stay home and look after my younger sister Liz and brother Tom. This I found rather to my liking but slowly all the housework was piled on the top of my other duties and Mrs. Hemming returned into my life by asking could I help her a little with their house.

This was arranged and I became a little drudge which improved neither my temper nor my ambitions. I remember very well the younger of the Hemming boys would invariably, if he knew I had gone upstairs for some reason, follow on some pretext or other, and way-lay me. I hated him the horrible boy and, like a little fool, never told anyone of his overtures for fear they would say "Of course it is that naughty bad girl again always making trouble."

Despite this, on Thursday afternoons when the chemist shop was closed and I had the house to myself, there was an interlude I loved. The drawing room was situated over the shop and on one wall stood a lovely upright piano and when I had washed all the lunch dishes I would steal a few minutes to seat myself at the instrument and try very hard to play that Scottish song 'Robin Adair'. I picked this because I realised it was simple. Before leaving school I had, despite my youth, reached the exalted standard of X7, and was given a smattering of music and French, hence my knowing that the piece I chose for my solitary piano recital was easy. After this I would resort to the kitchen, on one wall of which hung the telephone. An oblong contraption with a handle on one side and the speaker on the front but the hearing aid was separate and had to be held to the ear. I loved to wind the handle and hear the voice of the operator asking what name and number I wanted. Not knowing the name or number of anyone lucky enough to own one of these wonderful contraptions, I could only replace the ear piece but the thrill, the joy having someone interested enough in me to ask what number I wanted. This I invariably did every Thursday afternoon when my employers, if you could call them by this exalted name, for I only received one shilling and sixpence for my labours, would no doubt have gone to a matinee or to play bridge at the Conservative Club.

This arrangement only lasted six months for Sarah Ann informed us that she was trying to get a house, one with running water and gas. What a joy this was to be – no more going to the communal tap to fill the boiler, no more filling up the lamp with paraffin oil and, best of all, no more having to light the fire in the living room grate before you could have a cup of tea.

It was now that I was told that I must go out to work full-time in order to help pay for a front room suite and other luxuries we would need now that we had a parlour. So I was initiated into the mysteries of the Tan Yard of Thomas Bayley. Finished were my self-taught lessons on the piano, but not before I had tried in my youthful mind to make the family the possessor of one of these lovely instruments which not only produced music but also enhanced the draped beauty of any parlour.

It happened in this manner. One afternoon there was a persistent knocking on the front door of the terraced house in which we had now taken up our abode. Through the panelled glass door at the end of the passage I saw a man standing and on opening found a young well-dressed fellow of about twenty five or thereabouts. He enquired was my mother home, I replied no, but he informed me that he was from a German firm of piano makers and, as their representative, he was offering house-holders of good repute the chance to become owners of one of their wonderful overstrung, iron frame, upright instruments by immediately paying a small deposit, the rest to be paid in weekly instalments. What an opportunity! My dream could possibly come true! "Could you please call when my sister is home? I am sure she would be interested." Wishful thinking if you like! The man duly called to keep the appointment but, alas, failed to arouse any enthusiasm in Sarah Ann. How could we possibly afford such a thing? There were lots of things we needed before a piano. Everything in its proper turn.

Needless to say, we did have an instrument some years later and Sarah Ann was always sorry she had not taken advantage of the offer, for she found out later that the house-holders who had taken the bull by the horns and took on the weekly terms were eventually the proud owners of a wonderful German instrument not to be compared in any way with the British who, though excellent workmen and whose goods no country in the the world could hope to better, could in no way come up to the standard of the Germans as far as pianos were concerned. It was after about a year's payment had been made, and there were still many many more due, that the 1914 war was declared and the proud investors in owning a piano on weekly terms were literally presented with their purchases on a plate for, from the moment of hostilities being declared, they never paid another penny.

About a week before I started working at the Tannery, my brother Tom had the misfortune to set fire to the Hemming Warehouse. Although only eleven years old he had been doing odd jobs in the chemist's shop, such as serving paraffin oil, taking orders and delivering syphons of soda water.

On this particular evening about half past five I was busy washing up the dishes after the Hemming family had tea, there was no one there but myself, when a sharp hurried tap came on the door. On opening I found my brother standing on the step requesting a bucket of water which I immediately fetched and handed to him, then almost immediately a more hurried frantic knock and the request for more water. Naturally I asked what he was doing with the water? When he answered "The warehouse is on fire" I never hesitated for one moment not even to peer round the door to verify his statement. I dashed through the house into the very quiet sober atmosphere of the gentile chemist shop. Had it been a butchers or even a hardware emporium it would surely have not seemed so dramatic when in hushed but plainly audible voice I announced that the warehouse was on fire. The fire brigade was immediately called and it was in only minutes that Mr. Gaynor with brass helmet was attaching the hose he uncoiled from the engine which was drawn to the alarming scene by two stalwart horses. The engine came clanging down the street everyone dashing to reach the narrow pavements which bordered the fronts of the small terraced houses on either side.

As the bell clanged a feeling of doom entered my heart as I wondered what they would do to my dear brother. Could they send him to prison? Surely not; there must be some escape for him. I remembered the day when my father had knocked off the local police officer's helmet had my mother not appealed to Mr. Treece to tell the authorities that he, my father, was a law abiding citizen and that he had never been inside a police court let alone committed an offence. Treece being a well respected man owning the local laundry which traded under the name of Shaftesbury Laundry was a man to be relied on, and with his word that Dad was no hooligan who made a practice of interfering with the constabulary as did some of the rough cards of this time Dad was cautioned and warned that he must not let his enthusiastic exuberance interfere with others, particularly the wardens of the peace. But my dear mother was no longer here and who could we rely on to get my brother out of this dreadful predicament?

Tom was at this time not yet eleven years old. Could anything more ludicrous be imagined than to send a boy of these tender years into a warehouse which was a veritable trap. The floor was liberally strewn with straw to soak up any surplus oil spilt as the bottles or containers were filled from the huge vat which stood behind the door in this dark building which boasted no window and relied on the feeble gas jet over the paraffin tank. There were tins of paint and other inflammable stock and in the centre of this room stood a ladder which led to an upper room which was quite well lit by windows and was the home of Mrs. Hemming's prize canaries.

Imagine a small lad with a box of matches in his hand and a can waiting to be filled from the tank of inflammable oil. They do say "Familiarity breeds contempt" and Tom was quite conversant with this highly explosive situation but only once did he drop the lighted match but this was enough the whole place was an inferno in less time than it takes to write this description. Needless to say the poor canaries were all suffocated. The fire was eventually controlled and all is well that ends well, but it did not end well for me, although I never knew whether this episode in my brother's life upset him in any great degree.

I was a few years older than he and it was a great source of worry to me, and I would wonder if it was perhaps my fault that the canaries had died. Should I have rushed in with more water and tried to have quelled the outburst for it seemed an interminable time before the firemen arrived with their equipment?

Although I was still very young I knew that the Hemming's direct neighbours, a butcher on one side and the newsagents on the other, wasted no sympathy on the chemist and his family in their dilemma. In fact I was under the impression that they were probably pleased with the way fate had taken such a drastic step in bringing tragedy to both him and his wife.

Mrs. Hemming was, although kind in her way, a woman who could create that horrible feeling of inferiority in a person; she had a very superior manner with her, and having a very good share of female charm too, she was not liked by those who came into contact with her hourly, I was going to say daily, but it was more often than once a day that this small community met.

The shops which stood with their frontage on High Road opened out on a large tarmac yard, the far end being the old tub lavatories and the cycle sheds.

The sheds had a flat roof on which were boxes filled with soil and in the summer the chemist's wife grew nasturtiums, and of these her neighbours were dreadfully jealous. She knew this and on the slightest pretext would pick a quarrel, during which she would use the longest words in her vocabulary and both her neighbours were at a loss for words to retaliate both having had little education, so it was not to be wondered that no sympathy was wasted on such a stuck-up female.

The excitement of the fire died down and I believe the insurance was duly paid, although how this was made possible I shall never know for if ever there was a set up for a good conflagration there it was, in fact it could have been a death trap for a small boy as well as forty canaries. This situation would certainly not be tolerated today.

It was Friday morning when I started my first real job this being the day the week started in the Tanning Factory of Thomas Bayley & Son, Leen Gate, Lenton. I had passed this awful place many times before, in fact it was on the direct route to Nottingham, when one walked through Cut Through Lane, but I had not passed through the huge studded gates one must enter to gain access to the mysteries of the processing of animals skin into leather.

The outside of the grim establishment looked dark and dirty the windows in the compressed leather department were boarded half way up. This, I presume, was to stop vandalism but it did nothing to improve the dark, damp, smelly interior where about forty young girls and women toiled for ten hours every day clad in thick heavy shoes and a large leather apron to protect their clothing which, by the way, failed miserably, for one could not prevent some of the evil smelling concoction you worked with attaching itself to your blouse. It was a huge place one side having heavy long tables at which each girl was allocated about four feet of working space, standing in close proximity of each other, but never daring to speak for fear you would hear your number called out, with the order to go home for the day and the words "You have come here to work not to a party". Despite this there were moments when the overlooker would leave her point of vantage and some daring mortal would burst into song, though God knows what any of us had to sing about in these conditions.

The main heavy gates opened into a kind of archway and it was from this point the gatekeeper rang his bell, this being up in the belfry on the top of the buildings. It was rung every morning to signal us both in and out, if you were two minutes late after the clanging which could be heard quite a considerable distance away, you were fined three checks or the equivalent of three pennies. This we could ill afford and should the dreaded sound occur before we were near the gate we would run as fast as our legs could carry us to try to defeat its dreaded purpose. Once through the portals you were safe for the gatekeeper must lock them, this was one of the tasks. There was a glass top roof lean-to building which served as a cloakroom and dining room. At one end stood an old iron gas stove, no oven just open jets on the top which when covered with an iron plate was used for hotting up the dinners we carried in our baskets from home. For frying there was one iron frypan which we took in turns to use, as the occasion arose. We also took it in turns to light the stove and on Friday, after dinner, scrub the wooden tables we ate off; very rarely was the floor touched except for a quick sweeping and the walls of the place were festooned with spiders webs. So much for the dining room! The toilets were intricacies I never did understand for they were only flushed about once a day by some unseen method. These also we took turns to clean. For washing our hands there was a huge tank filled from the River Leen whose waters were used in the process of tanning – no towel or even rag to dry them on, no such luxury.

At seven a.m. we would start our daily round in the compressed leather shop. Some called it the compo shop, and others the knocking shop with a leering grin; the reason for this was that every girl was supplied with a large wooden mallet and a strong pair of scissors about ten to twelve inches long. These were her stock-in-trade without which she could not work. The mallet had an iron plate on the bottom and the shears were used to cut any thick skins.

The men started work at six a.m. and it was one of their tasks to wet the small skins, some of which were very small, one could never let imagination run riot, this would be too horrible. There was a huge vat filled with a boiling starchy liquid into which the bags of dried skins were emptied and allowed to impregnate for a period of time; they were then removed and drained on a huge slimey table from which they were weighed out. The girl would take the portion of slimey mess to her table on which was placed an iron frame, similar to a picture frame, measuring about twenty four inches by eighteen. There she would pick out the larger skins none of them more than four or five inches and stretch them on to the frame which stood on an hessian base. She would then proceed to fill in the centre of the frame with the pulpy mass left over, when this operation had been done she would take up the mallet and hammer the horrible mess until it was level and smooth, no holes left. Then she would turn in the edges of the layer on the bottom, the ends having been left over the rim of the frame in order to make a seal. This done she would proceed to place the skins left over on to the top of the layer of hammered pulp, this must be a neat operation otherwise the work was spoiled. Then she would dash to the press which stood on the other side of the room and take up a square flat tin the same size as the sheet of work she had made, return to her table and transfer the whole thing on to the tray, place her number on the work and rush over to the overlooker who could, if she so decided, tear up the whole construction, or send you back to your table to patch it up. If you were lucky you would reach the 'Old Gals' table (this name was a sort of endearment) before anyone was there, and be rewarded for your work by a check which was the equivalent of one penny. These you stored in a tin and every morning at eleven a.m. you would join the queue to hand them into the office where the 'Old Man' sat waiting. He entered the number of these checks into the book and the more you handed him the larger your pay on Friday evening.

On the work meeting with the overlookers approval it was placed in a huge press which took out all the surplus moisture and on removal was once more inspected by the foreman. Should the sheet of compressed leather not meet with his approval you were made to pay for it by forfeiting one check. Despite all this one became adept at the work and could earn very good wages which made up in a degree for the horrible job and terrible conditions we girls experienced. This was the only place in which the girls were working, except of course the offices, and there was quite a distinction in the status of the select few who managed to acquire work in the more select part of the building.

I remember well one Friday evening along with one of the girls, we were making our tired way home; it had been a sultry hot summer's day with a storm threatening all day and just before knocking off at six p.m. it broke. After some discussion we decided to make a dash for home, a matter of a good half hour's walk. We had just reached the top of the hill on Cut Through Lane when the storm reached its height. No sign of animal life, except of course we two weary girls plodding along, no sign of a bird, in fact everything silent as the storm reached its final crescendo, and towards the west a huge ball of fire came into our vision and a matter of yards away burst in a terrible explosion. This was too much. Frightened and hysterical we both turned on our heels and ran back down the hill, not daring to face this dreadful powerful phenomenon we had witnessed. Absolutely wet through with the torrential rain and shocked in no small way, for we were very young, we eventually decided to face the elements and make a dash for home.

This was the one and only time I have ever seen a thunder bolt and I have no wish to see another.

The motor car was gradually taking over from the horse-drawn carriage and Thomas Barton of Chilwell had about two charabancs on the road. These ran intermittently into town and back, but everyone still favoured the train service as a means of travelling to their work. The picture houses were springing up in every town, both in small places as well as the cities, and Beeston of course being a prosperous go ahead small urban town was not slow in acquiring two such places of entertainment. The first was the Palace which in its infancy was a cinematic entertainment shown in one of the rooms in the remains of the factory, which was reached by an entry which now stands between Parr's butchers' shop and Alex Owen's emporium. This was known as the Cosy Corner, but was, after a while replaced by a large tent, which in its turn was dismantled when the Palace was built on site where the Fine Fair supermarket now stands. About a year after an even more exciting building was erected and bore the title of the Palladium; this stood where the Tesco store now stands. Many was the time I have seen a full show for the princely sum of one penny and a heart ticket. These supplementary tickets were given by the local tradesmen. I always acquired mine at the laundry where I always took Dad's collar and front to be washed and starched every Monday morning and fetched it back on Saturday dinner, so one could say I was a regular customer. The transaction cost three half pence for both articles, and how white and crisp they looked in their brown paper bag!

Every Wakes Monday our Aunt Vina and Uncle Tom Whittaker would pay us a visit. She was my father's sister Lavina but we always called her Vina. Dad, along with all the other employees of Beeston Foundry, had his annual holiday this particular week but there was no holiday pay and the week following was a sad time, for the women folk had to supply for their families but had little money to accomplish the task.

My father's sister was a very good looking woman with a lovely head of golden hair the colour of ripe corn with a complexion usually associated with this coloured hair. Her husband was a smart man with a dark beard and moustache in the style of Edward the Seventh, very neat and trim. They were blessed with four children, two girls and two boys only one favouring their father the others auburn. My mother would never let Thomas Whittaker out-do my father in smartness. She always had a nice tailored suit made by Mr. Kirchins the local tailor for the working man, the moneyed folk favoured Mr. Thornhill who lived about four doors from Hemming the chemist. Both tailors lived on the High Road. Periodically we would visit my mother's brother John and his wife but their visits to our house were less frequent and I missed the lovely times my mother and her brother used to have when she was alive.

I was now in my teens and along with Flo and other friends I loved to take walks over the fields at Chilwell to Long Eaton and there we would enjoy talking to the local boys who would pair off with us and walk us back again. This procedure was on alternate evenings reversed and they would walk into Beeston and we would return as far as the Co-operative Store on Chilwell Road. What happy days these were! Horace Atkinson would play his mouth organ and we girls would sing along with such tunes as Moonlight Bay, Beautiful Doll, You Made Me Love You, not forgetting, If You Were The Only Girl. Jazz had just become popular and although my dad always alluded to the tunes and rhythm as "just trash" we loved the syncopated tunes such as Ragtime Cowboy Joe, Yiddle On Your Violin, Midnight ChooChoo. What happy times we had! On Sunday afternoon we would put on our summer dresses and make foursomes on the river, the boys rowing. What happy delightful innocent pastimes these were!

Everything was so lovely and innocent with no thoughts of the future. My favourite among all my friends was Flo, she was a happy carefree girl, always smiling and full of fun and jokes. The boys loved her and because she would do all those things I longed to do, but dare not, I loved her too. But oh! the trouble she would get me into. My sister Emily never did take to her and would never let me out if Flo came to call, "No" she would say, "Lottie has the dishes to wash" or some other task which would be quite true as we all had our tasks set out for us, but Flo would hang about for some appropriate moment when I could make a dash and join her, never caring what would happen until I had to face the music on my return.

Time went merrily on, for we were young with never a care; there were so many thing to enjoy. The Wakes, which was the first Sunday nearest to the eleventh of July, was a great occasion, full of frivolity. We would do the Turkey Trot and run one another around with confetti and tickler brushes. On the Sunday the men's clubs would walk to the parish church attended by the Silver Prize band, many of the marchers never entering the church again until the following year when the proceedings were repeated. On the Monday, the church Sunday Schools would walk from the old cross which stood were the war memorial is now. Before starting off they would invariably sing 'Stand up for Jesus' and 'Onward Christian Soldiers' then follow the procession along with drays decorated with Biblical Scenes for which the best had a prize. There were great days, so simple so happy!

It was in the month of June prior to the war being declared that Queen Mary and King George the Fifth made a visit to Nottingham, I remember well standing at the main gates of Wollaton Hall on Derby Road at the bottom of Hill Side to see them enter the grounds of the residence of Lord Middleton. How lovely she looked in an open Landau dressed in a lovely blue dress holding a small parasol over her head. It was a glorious day! Both Flo and myself had summer dresses on; mine was pink sprinkled with little blue rose buds, the skirt was draped. How I loved it! It really made me look good – the pale pink seemed to bring a little colour to my pale cheeks. I remember the material was fourpence three farthings a yard from Meakins and Lottie Harrison who had a small shop on CityRoad made it for me. That dress I shall never forget.

Life went on in a carefree way until August 4th 1914 when England declared war on Germany, not that this made much difference to us, except we saw the boys of the Staffordshire Regiment who had been billetted at Chilwell on the Militia ground march away but this did not worry us, or them, as the band played them down to the Railway Station; goodbye to the Royal Staffordshires.

Then came the war and Kitchener was appealing to the youth of the country to volunteer for service in the forces. With one accord these young and, I can truthfully say, innocent lads went to their doom, for many of them never returned. Poor lads they had no idea what they were going to and no more did we girls as we waved a dozen or more of them off on their adventure with the song, "Farewell Isabel". They were all in the local battalion 2/5 Sherwood Foresters and most of them stayed together. At first they were drafted to Ireland, where there was trouble and stayed until 1917, they were then sent to France and were only there seven days when they were sent to the front line at Ypres and, along with the rest of the 2/5, were practically wiped out; it was in this battle that I lost my first sweetheart, well shall I say second, for had not dear Harry been my very first as a child?

In April 1916 my workmate Polly and I decided we would leave the Tan Yard and get a job on munitions, Chilwell Shell filling factory was being built in the very fields we used to cross on our way to Long Eaton. The melting houses were filling the shells, but later a new method of pressing the dry T.N.T. into the shell was adopted which was quicker and more effective. It was a snap decision when we left the yard; the foreman had made both Polly and I return to sort the waste we made during the course of creating the compressed leather sheets. This was done periodically to keep all the girls on their tip toes and prevent undue waste. It was a most unfair procedure and everyone revolted at the system, time was wasted and with time money for the girls. So out we came and immediately walked from Lenton to Chilwell in fact Toton bend, where the temporary offices were situated. After some controversy about my age (I was only just seventeen and the authorized age was 18) I was taken on as an overhead crane driver. In the afternoon we returned to Lenton and collected our cards after some dispute, then walked home again. This involved about thirteen miles but this never worried us.

Along with about eight other girls we were taken over to the building later to be known as the filled shell store and to our consternation we were told we were to be trained to drive the overhead cranes which were suspended on rails on the roof of the building.

We could hardly believe our eyes! We had to ascend a ladder to man the crane and descend by way of a rope when descent was necessary. Imagine this! I was never very brave, but this procedure fairly took the cake. Here I was in a predicament I had never visualized; if I failed to mount the ladder I would be out of work and this I could not face. I had my board to pay so up I went, but it was some time before I mastered the rope.

My first impression of that store was sheer fright, rows and rows of 8in. 6in. and 9in. shells not forgetting the 12in. which reached to my waist and higher. I hardly dare walk near them, but had to overcome this feeling. As I remember it, I believe there were fifteen bays in the story and four cranes in each. On the lower side of the building there were two cranes to each bay and six large wall cranes. We were on eight hour shifts at first but this was changed to twelve hours. This meant two shifts instead of three. We worked twelve hours on Monday to Saturday, then we changed to eighteen hours, going on duty at 6 p.m. on Saturday and working until 2 p.m. Sunday when the opposite shift would take over and work through until Monday 6 a.m. when we would resume normal twelve-hour shifts. It really seems incredible now; no-one would work those long hours today or the Union would step in. Of course, this was war-time and everyone was out to get results. I remember that we were asked to join the Transport and General Workers Union and we did. I presume this was when everyone was becoming conscious of the need for unity even among the unskilled workers.

In December 1916 the factory was visited by King George the Fifth. The crane drivers put on a special loading of a convoy of 8in. and 9in. shells. The whole train of over thirty waggons was shunted into the building, loaded and shunted out in less than 8 minutes. It seems incredible! Loaders on the floor hooked on the shells, four 8 in. or three 9 in.; the drivers carried them to the trucks where the waggon loaders stacked them in the truck and they were away, via Newport, Monmouthshire, to the front. The party were most impressed but how these men perspired! Of course the pace could not be kept up indefinitely, but to see a convoy loaded even in ordinary time was quite a spectacle.

Sarah Ann was now married to Ernest and at home, young Ernest was born in 1916, the apple of his mother's eye. Lizzie was still at school a lovely girl, everyone loved her, she was such a sweet girl. Emily was courting her future husband George. Neither Ernest nor George had to do military service. Ernest had an accident down the pit and this incapacitated him for any service. George had a bad operation for internal trouble and this kept him out too.

It was about this time that my mind once more returned to the reason for death, so many young men were being killed in France and there seemed no end to the dreary days of war, and although I was only in my teens I realised the misery and anxiety this brought to families with men and boys of military age. My dear brother was too young for service but I could sympathise with the parents and young wives whose sons and husbands had answered the call of Kitchener for volunteers. Although all the men who fought did not offer their services and enlist in the forces, some were called in and had no option but to respond. All kinds of patriotic songs were sung and one would think that to die for one's country was as heroic a gesture as one could possibly make, to die for King and Country. What a complete waste of the darling youth of that era!

When I said my prayers, as we had always been taught, I would ask God to take them up to heaven, but I was beginning to wonder where heaven could possibly be, and if the entrance to this celestial place could not be made by an easier journey than blood, sweat, tears and terrible agonies of knowing that the man facing you was trying his best to help you along the path. Was life not sweet to both men? How could they be ready to die, most of them so very young, perhaps leaving wives and young children. Surely they did not want to go to heaven? My father had often said "No-one has come back to tell us what it is like, so no-one is in a hurry to take the journey." But still I wondered.

I was by now blossoming out and beginning to have more confidence, probably helped by the knowledge that I was capable of being as interesting and pretty as other girls of my age. It was about this time that I learned to dance and I loved it. Although these weekly hops as we called them were attended by lots of young people the teacher was quite an elderly man. Mr. Snow was his name and he would demonstrate the new dances with his daughter as partner. He was of medium height and quite slim, but so very elegant in his steps and gestures he was a pleasure to watch and I longed to emulate the free and easy way the couple moved their bodies. Despite the fact that a great majority of the young males were on active service we never seemed to be short of partners. Unlike the girls of today we would have thought it de-grading and not at all enjoyable to dance with a girl friend. Nothing could be more entrancing than to dance to the strains of the two piece orchestra, piano and voilin in the arms of a smart young civilian or maybe a darling soldier home from the front, for in those days a service man must always wear his uniform, it was against regulations to wear mufti.

The war was now in its fourth year and despite the suffering and rationing the country did put on a good face for the world to see, but the horrors of the war were brought home to everyone living in a fifteen mile radius of the Chilwell Shell Filling Factory in one dramatic and terrible moment. There had been several minor explosions – one in the Melt Houses where two men were killed – and we knew the TNT was mixed in the mills and taken to the Press House where the powder was pressed into the shell cases, and one would not fail to know the girls and men who worked in this part of the factory, for their hands and often their faces took on a dreadful yellow appearance, but despite this the terrible explosion that occurred on July 1st 1918 came as a shock to everyone.

There were two shifts at the factory A and B. I worked on A and it was B who caught the brunt, although it was said that the event had been intended for both shifts. The accident happened about 5 minutes to 7 p.m.. Had it been one hour previous the casualties would no doubt have been double for it would have caught the workers going off work and the relieving shift coming in.

On this particular evening I went home to find Emily had gone to the dentist. I had the evening meal she left for me and was washing the dishes at the kitchen sink when the terrible explosion happened. The day had been very hot and the window was wide open but the vibration blew it in and everything including the house moved. I looked up to the window and a huge mushroom spiral of smoke and debris was rising to the sky. For the moment I thought my dear sister was there at the scene. Why I should think this I shall never know but think it I did and, racing out of the house, I ran calling "Emily, Emily, Emily." The next thing I recall was someone saying who does she want? Is it Edna? By this time Emily and Sarah Ann had returned and Dad and Tom had joined us. Liz was with Emily and Sarah Ann. Like everyone we made our way towards the High Road. But what a scene of horror met us! Every available vehicle had been commandeered to take the casualties to the hospitals. Men, women and young people burnt, practically all their clothing burnt, torn and dishevelled, their faces black and charred, some bleeding with limbs torn off, eyes and hair literally gone. It was rumoured that it was possible the whole mixing house and mills would go up and Dad decided it would be best if we made our way to the fields, which we did, still hearing the carts, lorries and ambulances making their way with their gruesome loads to the hospitals. We came back home after midnight, but still the conveyances were making their way to Nottingham. The High Road, Beeston, had never before seen a cavalcade such as this and I hope, please almighty God, it never will again.

Next morning along with several of the other crane drivers I went to report for work, but the police would not allow us to pass through the main gates although we produced our permits. These permits took the form of a brass medallion about 2 inches across and bearing the entwined C's of the names of Viscount Chetwynd and the Chilwell Factory. But, not to be thwarted, we made our way along a narrow lane which ran on the extreme edge of the factory and on to a more elevated position from where we could see the horrible havoc that had occurred. The ambulance men along with volunteers were still searching for the buried in the ruins. We were told to return at 6 a.m. as usual on the Wednesday morning when as far as possible normal work would resume.

There was a great hole in the wall of the filled shell store and, as we travelled up and down in the overhead travelling cranes, we could see the rescue squads still at work. There were lorries piled high with unvarnished coffins, the last homes of those who were killed in such a sudden and horrible way. I believe there were about 120 mutilated corpses laid in the Church at Attenborough, most of them unrecognisable, others who were not so bad and who were identified by their relatives were buried privately.

The following Monday, along with other women and men, we represented the A shift of the Filling Store. Every work place had their own mourners, Filled Shell, Empty Shell, Melt Houses, Press Houses, Mills, Experimental House not forgetting clerical and canteen workers; this awesome cavalcade wended its way along Chetwynd Road and down Attenborough Lane to the strains of the works band playing the Dead March in Saul. This was before any houses had been built on Chetwynd Road and Attenborough Lane was so narrow a large cart could scarcely pass, so as the procession turned the corner from the main road, the whole scene would be witnessed at the main gates of the factory. But work soon resumed to normal and, strange to say, we none of us seemed to have any fear that there might be another of these dreadful scenes; the shells must be filled and the convoy sent on their way for things were very serious on all fronts.

Time went on, and we reached the day everyone had been hoping and praying for, the eleventh day of November 1918 when the armistice was signed, and thank God we did, when the news came through. A shift was on the day turn and precisely at eleven a.m. we were all told to assemble on the lawn. This was a huge green space complete with band stand, where we would congregate after our mid-day meal to listen to the band or to dance according to the music played, but there was a difference on this day. The band were assembled with full uniforms and bright instruments and seated also was Lord Chetwynd and other dignitaries from the War Office. The main speech was made by Chetwynd himself and we were all thanked for the part we had played in helping to bring the desired results over four years of war. Never before had any factory been given the title of the **V.C. Factory.** Now we were told the war was over and we could all resume our previous roles of living an individual life, the band played and we all sang that beautiful old hymn "Oh God our help in ages past, our hope for years to come." A fitting finale for a stirring occasion.

As soon as the strains had died away everyone was making an effort to get away from the scene as quickly as possible in order to make the most of the remainder of the day. I was never very nimble in my actions, always inclined to clumsiness and for this reason I failed to jump on one of the lorries that were being commandeered to help in the swiftest possible retreat from the confines of the factory that had held us captive for three years, with never one single moment to relax from our twelve hours daily and eighteen hours on change-over duties at the week-end making our normal working week 80 hours. The weather was perfect for the time of year and a more fitting day could not be expected, away we all went to revel in our simple pleasures. A job well done.

We all returned to work the following morning knowing full well that it was only a matter of time before we would all be looking for work in other spheres. Those who had jobs to return to were quickly offering themselves to their previous employers, others like Polly and myself had burnt our boats when we walked out that morning in March over three years ago. We could hardly return to our former work, so we played the waiting game and lingered on, knowing that any day could be our last at the V.C. Factory. It was not long before the Army Ordnance took over the factory, everything was dismantled and the whole place turned into a depot for returned equipment of army stores, such as saddles, canteen accessories, etc. We were given the task of cleaning the leather equipment and sorting the other returned utensils etc. The staff was slowly diminishing and we were more or less waiting our turn to be demobilised.

In April of that year 1919, my sister Emily had her first child Irene and I absented myself from work to look after her and her house where I was living at the time in Stapleford. During this time I accidently scalded my foot which necessitated my having more time from the factory than I had anticipated when applying for leave, and no doubt in my case this was one of the deciding factors in my dismissal which followed almost immediately on my return to work.

We, that is two of my work mates also crane drivers and I, were working on saddles over by the stores offices and decided that to eat our lunch would be a good idea and immediately set to doing just that. To our dismay our names were suddenly called out and we were told to report at the Big Head Office and collect our insurance cards where we were instantly dismissed for eating in a restricted area.

This rule was made during the days of the factory's role as a TNT filler of shells and, as this particular powder was a poison, no one was allowed to eat in the precincts of any of the factories workshops, but we were not now in a situation where this applied, no shells having been filled since Armistice Day. Despite this we were given our cards much to our distress; we cried all the way up to the office to receive our dismissal. This was a good an excuse as any for removing us from the pay roll and making us reliant on the dole, which was at this time £1. 5s. 0d. From this princely sum we must pay our board and lodgings for in these days no person of any principle at all would allow their parents to keep them – it was not done.

May, Sarah and myself were just four days looking for work, Sarah and May returned to the lace trade, but I took on myself a new role as a machinist in the making-up trade.

Chapter 3 TOWARDS A NEW LIFE

I was now twenty years old and, as I thought, very experienced in worldly matters, for had I not worked with women twice my age who were well voiced both in experiences in and out of the marriage vows? My upbringing had always been, both with and under the guidance of my mother as with my two elder sisters, not strict or hard, but a discipline that was tempered with love and understanding. We were taught right from wrong and the pit-falls that came with mixing with 'wrong-uns'. So it was little wonder and no particular credit to myself that I never, despite nearly four years working side by side with some of the roughest, walked down the road with any man. Lots of the girls did take up with married men and, according to the reports they gave us less venturesome mortals, a grand time they had for lots of men were drafted into the factory under the Lord Derby Scheme, when a man could be taken into any work that was designated for him. Like the armed forces they had to leave wives and home behind, although quite a lot of them did continue to make homes for the families they had been forced to leave, but others the arrangements suited and they were the ones who were looking for easy fry to pass their time with.

So although I never indulged in any of the practices which were so easy to enter, I knew the downfalls that could occur should a girl be foolish enough to fall into the trap. I had come out of the fray as I went in and thanked God for it.

So on this particular day I walked into Nottingham in search of work – in fact determined to get a job. I had walked through Cut Through Lane and caught the tram at Sherwin Road alighting at Wilford Road. I crossed the Castle Boulevard and there it was, the job, on a big door at the junction of Wilford Road and Canal Street at the firm of Cox and Son was a notice:–

"Machinists wanted for neck wear and tea aprons."

I stood for a few moments wondering if I could possibly call myself a machinist. Of course I thought I could! I could treadle the sewing machine at home and had done ever since it was initiated into the family by my mother who had bought it prior to her death at a shilling a week. Wonder of wonders was this machine – it opened up a new world for us. Emily made herself a lovely dress in grey with white collar, the quaker girl style. The operetta 'The Quaker Girl' was very popular at this time and very lovely was the music. One song went like this, "I like your apron and your bonnet, and your little quaker gown, your manners so demure, as your modest eyes look down." and so on. So Emily was exceedingly pleased with her efforts at dress making but, for myself, I never remember making a solitary thing. Despite this, I knew I could work that old treadle machine, so up the stairs leading from the big dirty door I went. Up the stone steps and into an office, where a woman was sitting. "Can you machine?" "Yes of course." "Well then, start on Monday morning." So away I went thinking of nothing except that I had a job.

I remember distinctly washing the white blouse, the only one I had, in preparation for my initiation into the making up trade – the name given to all branches of the production of ready made clothing which was just coming into its own for prior to this time people had looked down on factory produced garments. Almost every street had its own particular dressmaker, in fact these producers of so many styles and fittings became experts in their own field and the public would place their own particular value on articles of clothing made by the tailoress, whatever this meant, but the truth was the snob value went up a hundred per cent if one could only truthfully say that Miss or Mrs. So and So had designed and made the creation you were wearing.

So here I was entering this very elite profession despite the fact that it was the humblest of entries, tea aprons and neck wear. I never saw any neck wear being made, the garments we produced were camisoles and aprons. The camisoles were flimsy creations of lace and cambric which the female wore over the bust of the wired corset fashionable at this time, when complete they were threaded with blue or pink velvet ribbon. A girl had to assemble and make twelve of these feminine frivolities for the princely sum of one shilling.

I remember very well my first entry into that room – the sewing machines all whirring away at a terrific speed and every back bent over the work in hand. I soon knew why, when I learned the rate one was paid for a dozen! Imagine my horror when I learned the machines were electrically driven! Nothing like the treadle we had at home, but despite my dire ignorance I quickly picked up the easiest way of manipulating the work to my advantage. I stayed at this place of work for about twelve months, then trade slumped and we went on short time, so despite the fact that I liked the work, I had to look for a job with a better pay packet. I had to travel by train and this took money apart from the fact that one had to dress that little better when one worked in town, so my career in the rag trade ended. Nevertheless in after years I was always pleased I had had this simple tutoring in sewing for it came in very useful as things turned out.

Emily had gone to live at Stapleford when she married and, at her invitation, I had gone to live with her but I went back to Beeston when I got work in Nottingham. In this way I defeated some of the worry concerning travel although as I remember the rate per mile was only one penny, it made a considerable difference when the distance was three times that of the journey from Beeston to Nottingham.

So after several weeks of struggling with the short time, Emily got me work in a local hosiery factory and once more I went to Stapleford to live. This time I was initiated into the mysteries of the hosiery trade. I never knew before this that socks and stockings were joined at the toe by an operation known as linking. The knitted articles came off the huge machines separated at the toe and it was the job of the linker to pick up every stitch onto a huge flat plate-like contraption which had on the extreme outside edge an array of sharp needles. The linker placed every separate stitch on to these needles while the machine was rotating. As it went round in a circular movement, at a given point a small knife cut off the surplus leaving a lovely neat toe. Now this may sound all very easy but believe me there were snags such as missing a stitch or the knife not cutting enough to make a neat job or worse still cutting to close and destroying the toe.

There were days when everything went well and one could literally gallop along but oh those awful days when one had to call for help from the mechanic! In these conditions no-one worried but the linker and she poor dear had just to wait. No pay, no sympathy and probably a warning that this kind of thing could not be tolerated. You were there to work. But once one became experienced the money was good although the work was tedious.

So my life began to settle down to its new pattern, and it was not to be long before I would meet up again with the man I would marry but in the months after the war that was not on my mind. We were thanking God that as a family we had survived the War. Then out of the blue, our beloved little brother dropped his bombshell. He was only just seventeen but he had decided to join the army and had already done so.

What horror, what heartache! The apple of Sarah Ann's and Emily's eyes! They were both horror struck. We could not believe that after the horrors of the Great War he would consider joining the Army. I remembered that in the summer months before the war the militia (The Territorials of Notts. & Derbys.), would camp at Chilwell on Hallams Lane and the corner of Bramcote Lane. They always looked so smart in their red jackets, striped trousers and pill box hats complete with cane. But Dad hated us to go over to the field as many of the public did on Sunday afternoons and we were forbidden. He always said that in private life they were rag and bone men and other professions of ill-repute, in fact wasters, and on the top of this they were only butterfly shooters. But one afternoon it had come to his ears quite accidentally that Tom had not been at Sunday School, not that he really cared one way or the other about this, but Tom must have openly defied him and gone over to the Militia ground. Father set off in a rage to find Tom, which he did, coming along Chilwell Road. In the distance Tom saw Dad waiting and knew there was no escaping him for he stood patiently waiting with the leather belt he had taken from round his waist in his hand. Round the monument which stood in Post Office Square they went, Tom always a little out of reach. This was the only time I ever knew Dad to hit him. Remembering this, we felt sure that Dad would support us in helping to secure Tom's release from the army.

It was a cold Tuesday evening in January when I went to see Dad but he would not listen to my plea. We, that is Emily, Sarah Ann and myself, only asked for support, no money – we would raise that ourselves in an attempt to free our dearest of brothers from his own foolhardiness – but Dad would have none of it. He could only say "He has made his bed and he must lie on it; it will make a man of him". Despite lack of co-operation from Dad and the delight of young sister Lizzie who said "He has given me many a hard punch. I'm glad he's gone." we decided to write to his commanding officer.

This job fell to me and subscribing a very pathetic letter informing him that our brother was only just seventeen years of age and if this could not be classed as a reason for him not being accepted, then we were prepared to buy him out.

Of course we were ignored but my father received a letter informing him that to all intents and purposes his son was eighteen years of age and because it was his desire personally to make the Army his career there was nothing more to be said. You can never imagine the awful despondency caused by this abrupt dismissal.

After this every Friday evening was spent in making jam tarts, swiss puddings and mince pies which were despatched in a tin box to be received at Catterick Camp on Monday morning; Sarah Ann would run up to the Post Office with the parcel every Saturday morning.

It was weeks before we saw him and then, joy of joys, the letter arrived to say that he was coming home on furlough. No-one was prouder than the Martin family that day. Dad, poor old man, shed a few surreptitious tears and Sarah Ann ridiculed him for doing so. My brother made a perfect figure of a man, or shall I say 'boy', for he stood seventeen years of age, six foot four inches in his stockinged feet and every inch a soldier. Was there any prouder man in the world when at sixty years of age and an old soldier himself, my father picked up his son's pack on his shoulder and walked to Beeston station to see his son off to Catterick after his first leave! He had a gleam in his eye never to be seen again.

POSTSCRIPT

After my grandmother's death in 1976, the family discovered that unbeknown to us, she had spent some time in her last years writing down her early memories. It was clear that she intended to write more but illness in her last years must have prevented this. Although incomplete as an autobiography – for my grandmother faced many more troubles in her life – I was delighted that she left this description of her early years and I hope that you have enjoyed reading it as much as I did.

Like many other people of her generation, she had a very hard life especially after her husband died in 1937 leaving her with a family to bring up on her own. To make ends meet she took cleaning jobs but somehow managed to attend night classes and eventually achieve her ambition of becoming a cookery teacher.

The hardship of my grandmother's life never embittered her. On the contrary, she was a warm-hearted, generous and sensible person who was adored by her family and admired by her friends. She had grown to these strengths in spite of the rigours of her life – indeed she would have said because of them. As she often used to say

"Suffering and hardship build character"

Paula Hill

Lottie 1964

APPENDIX

Lottie wrote the following notes on her family background:

My grandmother Ann Smith was born in the year 1829 at Tewkesbury where my grandfather Joseph Pardoe was also born two years later. They were married at the Parish Church there in 1851. There were three children of the marriage who survived and my mother was the youngest. She was born on the 18th April 1862 at Smith's Yard, a narrow road off the High Street leading to the River Avon, and was registered Rebecca Pardoe. The other children were named John and Sarah. My mother lived with her family at Tewkesbury until she was seven years of age when they moved to Chesterfield where my grandfather was employed in the hosiery trade teaching the art of knitting by machine, he being an expert hand at this way of making stockings. Eventually the family moved again and came to Nottingham but my grandmother was to die young and left my mother at only ten years old; the dreaded scourge of consumption for which there was no cure in those days claimed her.

After this my mother was shuttlecocked from her sister to her brother like a parcel, her name and future destination being tied around her neck on a label. When she was about ten and a half years old she was sent to work in a silk mill. She was so small she had to stand on a box so that she could reach to perform the job she was set to do. At this time she went to live with her sister Sarah and often she would be left to attend the younger children of her sister's family. Life was very hard but despite this she always remembered to thank God for any blessings she received and to ask for strength to go about her life in the way her mother would have wished.

When she was about twenty years of age she met Thomas Martin who was at this time serving his apprenticeship as a brass moulder. His was a Roman Catholic family and I believe that his grandparents had come to England from Ireland during the great potato famine bringing his family with him. There were five children in the Martin family – Ann, Lavinia, Henry, Philip and my father Thomas who, like my mother, was the youngest of them. His father had died and his mother had a very hard life as a widow.

However it was some years before they married. My father went to work for a travelling show with roundabouts but he did not stay long with them and eventually joined the army in the Shropshire Light Infantry. Neither my mother nor my father's mother had any idea where he was and my mother told us in after years that our grandmother had died of a broken heart after my father disappeared. However I later came to understand that she had fainting attacks and it was during one of these bouts that she fell downstairs and this hastened her death.

While in the Army, my father was eventually sent out to Egypt to fight in the war with the Mahdis from 1882 to 1885. My mother heard nothing of him until one day in 1885 as she was leaving work in the evening she was surprised to see him waiting for her at the steps of the factory. They married in 1886 in Nottingham.